THE Spirit WITHIN ME

The *Spirit* Within Me

An Autobiography

Pamela Meintel

© Copyright 2017 by Pamela Meintel

All rights reserved. No part of this book may be used or reproduced without the express written permission of the author other than short quotations for articles and reviews.

I have tried to recreate events, locales and conversations from my memories of them. In order to maintain their anonymity in some instances I have changed the names of individuals and places, I may have changed some identifying characteristics and details such as physical properties, occupations and places of residence.

Printed in the United States of America

ISBN Paperback: 978-1542731522
ISBN eBook: 978-0-692-83698-9

Book Design: Ghislain Viau
Cover Artwork: Cathy Walker

Contents

Chapter 1 — The Spirit Within Me 1

Chapter 2 — Innocence Lost 9

Chapter 3 — Leaving the Small Town 21

Chapter 4 — Moving On 35

Chapter 5 — Devastating News 39

Chapter 6 — Living With Cancer 45

Chapter 7 — Staying True 51

Chapter 8 — Back to School 55

Chapter 9 — The Proposal 61

Chapter 10 — Life Changing Event 65

Chapter 11 — The Uncertainty 67

Chapter 12 — My Faith 71

Chapter 13 — The Journal 73

Chapter 14 — Waking Up 103

Chapter 15 — The Long Road To Recovery. 107

Chapter 16 — Going Home. 115

Chapter 17 — The Setback 119

Chapter 18 — Finding Strength. 125

Chapter 19 — July 4th. 129

Chapter 20 — Visiting. 137

Chapter 21 — Hands. 141

Chapter 22 — Post Parkinson and Dystonia. 145

Conclusion. 149

Acknowledgments 153

CHAPTER 1

The Spirit Within Me

I have found that sometimes we have to fall to the depths of our own personal Hell before we can get back up with a fresh new start. A physical and mental pain that could, in some cases, destroy and break one's spirit to the point of no return.

There were times I felt like I was in Hell, as though every inch of me ached in pain, a pain that lasted far too long. Then suddenly life is good again and you wonder why God would put you through all of that pain. Well, it isn't always just on God. Sometimes it's also on us.

I believe that God gives us the ability to make decisions that affect our own lives. There are many times in our lives where we choose our own destiny by the decisions we make.

The Spirit Within Me

With life's glorious sunlight shining down on me, I look at things so differently now. I have a new perspective of why we are here on this beautiful planet called Earth. I believe each and every one of us was put here for a purpose. That purpose may be revealed at a very young age without even realizing it. Or, it may come later in life, like it did for me.

Life has many mysteries. Some we are able to solve and some live on as a mystery forever. It is the unknown that is most difficult to live with. We often say, "If I only had a crystal ball I would know exactly what to do." Wouldn't that make life so simple? But if that were the case, what would we learn while we were here on Earth? We learn and grow from our mistakes, which in turn makes us better human beings.

My story tells of the many times when I could have given up and given in. Any one of these obstacles could have taken me down a dark path of no return. Instead I chose a different path and through my faith and strong will, I survived.

I have many fond memories of growing up in a small town. I had a younger sister and a younger brother; my sister Brenda is only two years younger than me, so we were very close growing up.

When I was three years old my parents bought me a pony named Jingles. He was an adorable looking black and white Shetland. I would brush him and feed him whenever I could. When I was 5-years old I was allowed to ride Jingles.

One winter, when I was 7-years old, my dad built a sled for Jingles to pull. We couldn't wait to try it out. One Sunday Dad got my cousins, my Aunt Linda (who was two years older than me), Brenda and me together to go for a sleigh ride. We were on my paternal grandparents' farm where there was a large open area covered with a snow-white blanket of snow which led to the woods. All us kids had just barely gotten on the sled when Jingles started to run, and when I say run, I mean full speed ahead. My dad tried to gain control of the reins, but Jingles would have nothing to do with that. At that point my dad began to panic. He was looking at a sled with five small children on it barreling towards a heavily wooded area. He yelled for everyone to jump off the sled as Jingles kept running straight towards the woods.

One by one all of the kids jumped off of the sled, except for me. I was so scared that I just froze. My dad was screaming for me to jump off, but I just couldn't get up the courage to do it. The sled was going so fast. I could feel the cold wind blowing on my face. I was just terrified. Jingles continued to head toward the woods with my dad running behind, but he couldn't catch up to us. As I looked back at my dad, the fear on his face terrified me and led me to believe that something horrible was about to happen.

Shortly after, we entered the woods. We were flying through the snow, barely missing several trees. I was scared to death. I knew that if I fell off, I would be seriously injured. I also thought that my dad would never find me.

Jingles finally came to an abrupt stop. I was so happy that I could finally get off of the sled. When my dad caught up to us, he promptly scolded me and then gave me a big hug. I am sure my dad just had the scare of his life. I couldn't have been happier to see him.

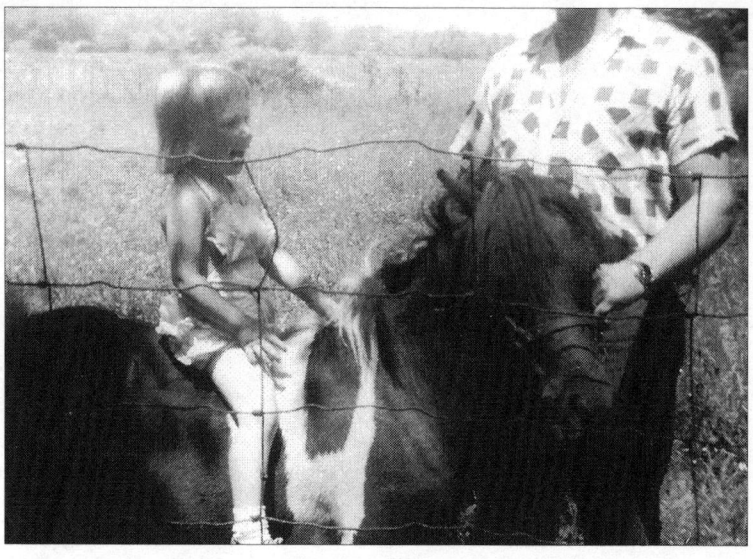

As children, my cousins Claudia and Randy, my Aunt Linda, and my sister and I would often get together and play. We would build forts in the woods, have sleepovers, and in the summer we would camp out in the pasture. We sat around a campfire and roasted hot dogs and marshmallows before heading to our tent for a series of ghost stories. Oh, how we loved to scare ourselves.

In the fall, my paternal grandpa would take the leftover apples from his orchard to a place where they had an apple press. He had the apple juice put into a large barrel, and a few weeks later we had apple cider. The barrel was situated in the backyard for easy access. We would put our glass under the spout and voila, we had a nice big glass of cold cider. As time went on, the cider would get more and more potent. We called it "hard cider," even back then.

As many families did during that era, our family lived close by my grandparents, aunts, uncles and cousins. I can still remember going to my paternal grandmother's house and smelling bread baking in the oven, while she fried green tomatoes on the stove. I loved to go there. She was always entertaining us with ghost stories. The stories scared us to death, but we always begged for more.

My grandmother was so warm and loving. She was exactly what a grandmother should be. My paternal grandfather was always playing jokes on us. He was a funny man. He was full of love and kindness, and I adored him. The fond memories that I have of both of my paternal grandparents will be with me for the rest of my life.

My dad liked to entertain, so he would host the holiday parties and picnics at our house. We had so much fun getting together with our family. Christmas was my favorite time of the year. My parents always hosted a Christmas Eve party.

The Spirit Within Me

All of our relatives would show up around five o'clock and we would have dinner followed by opening gifts. Then we would all sit around the fireplace and sing Christmas carols. It all just seemed so magical.

We took a family vacation every summer. One year, when I was 16 years old, we took a five week vacation out west. We traveled from Ohio to California and down into Mexico. We visited Mount Rushmore, Yellowstone Park, the Grand Tetons, and Disneyland. We even met Pancho Villa's widow while we were in Mexico. My poor parents had to listen to my sister and I complain the whole trip. At our age we would have much rather been home with our friends than traveling the country.

All in all, I had a great childhood.

I couldn't wait for school to end every summer so I could play with my sister and cousins. We lived on 20 acres, so there was always plenty to do. We had a small pond in our front yard so we would go swimming almost every day. The pond was stocked with fish that we would catch and eat. We would pull out our fishing rods and would always catch more than we needed for dinner. To this day I can't believe I was able to put a live worm on a hook. That is something I could never do today.

During my childhood I had a secret that no one was allowed to know.

A secret that my dad and mom didn't even want me to share with anyone outside of our immediate family.

CHAPTER 2

Innocence Lost

When I was 4 years old, my maternal step-grandfather began to molest me and my sister Brenda. He was determined not to get caught. He would often take us into his bathroom where he would remove his pants and have us fondle him when nobody else was home. Once he drove us down a desolate road near some railroad tracks where he would stop the car and proceed to molest us one at a time. He would remove our panties and then he inserted his fingers into our vaginas.

I remember feeling as though something was wrong with what he was doing, but I wasn't quite sure. I was very confused. Part of me knew it was wrong, but because of my age, another part of me thought that maybe, just maybe, it

The Spirit Within Me

was normal. He was the adult, so I trusted him. Besides, he was my grandpa, so in my mind I didn't think he would ever do anything to hurt us.

I do remember him swearing us to secrecy. It was a way for him to manipulate us so that we wouldn't tell anyone. I am unable to remember a lot of the various places he took us to, but for some reason the bathroom and the railroad tracks stayed with me.

The molestation went on for a year until one day, when I was five, I decided to go to my mom and dad and tell them what was happening. I needed to know if what he had been doing to my sister and me was okay. My parents were extremely upset when I told them. They hustled my sister and me into the car and drove us to my grandparent's house to confront my step grandfather. I remember feeling so uncomfortable and afraid of what would happen. There we were, my sister and I, standing before my parents and grandparents about to tell our long kept secret. My sister was only three years old at the time, so she did not take part in the conversation. It was up to me to try to tell what had taken place.

As it turned out, my step-grandfather denied everything. He said that I was making the whole story up. He couldn't believe I had accused him of such horrible acts. He denied everything up one side and down the other.

Innocence Lost

I couldn't believe my ears. Did he just say that he hadn't done those things to us? He stood right there in front of my sister and me and lied about everything. At my young age I didn't understand that adults were capable of lying. I thought that they always told the truth.

My grandmother was very angry with me. She said that if she believed me for one minute she would leave him. However, she would be staying with him because she believed we were lying. I knew from that day forward I would have to keep things to myself because no one would believe me. I didn't want to cause any more trouble than I already had. It seemed as if everyone was upset with me. It was a helpless feeling, just knowing that everyone thought that I had lied just to get my step-grandfather into trouble. My parents scolded me and said I should never tell a lie. My parents were probably embarrassed over the situation.

Because he was a master manipulator, and he knew that nobody would ever believe us, the molestation continued for 2 more years. All I could think of was that I couldn't protect my sister from this monster. She later reminded me of a time when he was coming up our driveway and we ran to the cornfield and hid, in hopes that he wouldn't find us. Thankfully, he thought that no one was home, so he left.

Years later, I realized that the molestation actually brought my sister and I closer, as strange as that might sound. We shared something that no child should share, but it became a bond between us. We both felt the negative emotions that one feels after being so violated. We could truly relate to one another.

When I was 10 years old I had a conversation with a female cousin. I found out that she was being molested by my step-grandfather as well. He did this during the same time that he molested my sister and me. I was also told by a neighbor girl of my step-grandfather that she had been molested by him as well. I don't know if these girls ever told anyone what had happened to them. If so, apparently nobody believed them either.

Innocence Lost

My sister and I were subjected to visiting my grandparents over the years and into our adult lives. I used to hate having to greet my step-grandfather. When I was 16 years old he would kiss me on the mouth and slip his tongue into my mouth. He did this to me until the day he died. I believe he counted on me to say nothing, and it worked.

As a young adult living in Arizona, with him living in Ohio, it was rare that we saw each other. Just being near him repulsed me. I was just too afraid to call him on it. I didn't want to go through all the embarrassment of having him deny it again. I had to behave as if nothing had ever happened, so I put a smile on my face and pretended to love my step-grandfather and grandmother. I felt that it was necessary in order to keep the peace in the family. It was all a facade in order to hide my true feelings. I despised the man.

I can't remember when the molestation actually stopped. I think it stopped when I was 7 years old.

My step-grandfather was married to someone prior to marrying my grandmother. His first wife and two young children were killed in a house fire. I always wondered if he had molested his own children and had gotten caught, forcing him to do the unthinkable.

We will never know, but I think it is a real possibility.

Years later I was told by a therapist that sexual predators choose a certain age group to prey on. Based on this, I believe my step-grandfather actually chose a younger age, knowing that nobody would believe them if they exposed him. It was a way for him to have total control over his victims. He had them believe that they must keep the secret. The girls that my step grandfather molested were all so young, vulnerable and easily manipulated. We were easy prey.

This also explains why he never molested my mother. She was 13 years old when he and my grandmother got married. With her being older, he felt vulnerable to getting caught. Because he didn't molest my mother, she had a hard time believing that he had molested my sister and me.

As a young adult I blamed myself for many years. I wondered if I had been promiscuous in some way, leading him to do the horrible things that he did. What could I have done to cause this man to harm my sister and me in the way that he did? As a 5 year old girl, I had many questions about this thing called, "molestation." Unfortunately, the answers didn't come to me until much later in life.

I felt a lot of guilt for causing my family so much grief after exposing my step-grandfather. Again, it wasn't until years later that I realized that I wasn't to blame. I was a victim of a sexual predator who had his own agenda and knew exactly what he was doing. He died in 1985 when I was

30 years old. He never did any jail time, which is a travesty. Someone as evil as he was needed to be stopped. He was a serial molester. How many more victims could there be? Innocent little children who had their childhood taken from them by one very sick man. I am sure he is getting what he deserves in Hell.

I couldn't blame my parents for not believing me about the molestation because they were so young, and in the early 60's the subject of molestation was taboo. It was just something that wasn't talked about.

When I was in my late thirties, my dad and I were sitting around talking about my childhood. I brought up the subject of when I was molested and went into some of the details. As an adult I was able to verbally communicate the details of what happened to me. My father was in shock. He told me that he thought that I mistook my Grandfather's hugs and kisses for something sexual. My father was extremely upset and began to cry as he apologized over and over for not believing me. I told my father they had no way of knowing because my step-grandfather was a master manipulator.

I always wanted my maternal grandmother to love me and care about me the way my paternal grandmother did. However, she wasn't the loving kind. In fact, she would intentionally say extremely mean things to me. She would say things like, "When are you going to get rid of some of that lard?" She too had her own agenda, and that was to make everyone around her miserable.

I feel that my grandmother knew exactly what was going on with my step-grandfather and the molestation. She treated me badly throughout my childhood and into my adult life. She despised me because I exposed her sexual predator husband. Part of me believes that she was just a bitter old woman who had no friends and could show no love to anybody.

When my mother was a baby, my grandmother sent her from Ohio to Tennessee to live with her grandparents until the age of seven, when they became too old to care for her. At that point she was sent back to Ohio and placed in foster care. My grandmother claimed she was unable to care for her financially. My mother remained in foster care until she was 17 years old. The entire time, my grandmother would only see my mother on weekends. Back then, in the 1940's, children in foster care were allowed to visit their parents.

One weekend when my mother was 12 years old, she visited my grandmother. My mother was talking on the telephone when my grandmother told her to hang up the phone. My mother wasn't quick enough, so my grandmother hit her over the head with the phone. Back then phones were extremely heavy, so the phone split my mother's head open. My grandmother ended up putting her into a taxi cab, alone, and sent her to the hospital. Once there, my mother told the doctor that she fell down some stairs and hit her head. She didn't want to get my grandmother in trouble.

My mother tried so hard to get her mother to love her, but to no avail.

There wasn't anything my mother could do to make my grandmother love her, it just wasn't in her. My mother was in her sixties when my grandmother passed. She never stopped trying to make things right with my grandmother, but she never could. As a daughter, I couldn't imagine being treated the way my mother was treated.

When I was in my thirties, my therapist recommended that I write my grandmother a letter, letting her know how I felt. It was a therapeutic way for me to let go of the pain that I felt over the years. Several years after my step-grandfather had passed on, I wrote the letter. I told her that I believed that she knew that her husband had molested me. In addition, I told her that it was a miracle that my mother turned out to be such a wonderful mother. She certainly didn't have a role model to follow. Lastly, I told her that I thought she was evil. I felt that any grandmother who would treat their daughter and granddaughters the way she did, had to be evil.

The letter upset my grandmother so much that she threatened to file a lawsuit against me for slander. She never did file the lawsuit. I assume she went to the attorney's office and he told her that she didn't have a leg to stand on. She ended up making copies of the letter and threatened to post them around my hometown. She never did that either.

The molestation was something that haunted me for most of my life with adverse effects. Unfortunately, I didn't realize it until many years later while I was in therapy. The molestation was a contributing factor in why I was overweight as a child and also contributed to my two failed marriages. I ate to mask the pain and by doing so I gained so much weight that I didn't feel good about myself. I felt as though I had to settle for something far less than I actually deserved. It was nothing more than a vicious cycle that lasted for years.

I am embarrassed to say this, but when I got a call in 1985 that my step-grandfather had passed away from lung cancer, I celebrated. I hoped that he had suffered an excruciating death. I hoped that he thought about the things that he did and that he had regrets as he lay there dying. In my mind, finally, I could move on and never have to face that evil man again. I was finally free.

Though part of me wished I would have confronted him as an adult.

I would have made him face the horrible things that he did, not only to me and my sister, but to all of the other girls as well. He should have had to pay for what he did.

To this day I refer to my step-grandfather and grandmother by their first names, Baldy and Opal. They don't deserve the title of "Grandpa and Grandma."

This was the beginning of the tests that God would lay out for me to overcome.

CHAPTER 3

Leaving the Small Town

Four days after I graduated high school, in 1974, I headed to Phoenix, Arizona with two of my high school friends. I was always independent, so leaving home was no problem. I couldn't wait to begin my journey.

One thing I didn't count on was being terribly homesick; I missed my family and my friends so much that it hurt. I did my best to overcome it and get on with my new found freedom.

Eventually I settled into my new life and started enjoying being independent. While I was in Phoenix I decided to go to the Bryman School to become a dental assistant. It wasn't college, but it was a trade that I knew I would enjoy.

When my friends and I moved to Phoenix we didn't have a car, so we had to take the bus everywhere we went. I went to school during the day and worked at a department store in the evening. There were days when we didn't have anything to eat but a bag of popcorn. It was difficult, but I think it made me appreciate everything a little more. I was now on my own and had to survive, one way or another. I loved my independence, so it was all worth it in the end.

While I was in Phoenix, I met a man who would become my first husband. He was also from Ohio which instantly drew me to him. We seemed to have a couple of things in common. We both loved sports and it was the first time either one of us had had a girlfriend or boyfriend. Two years later we were married.

As most girls do, I always dreamed of a big wedding in my home town. A wedding with all of my friends and relatives there, to enjoy the day with us. As a little girl, I pictured myself walking down the aisle in a beautiful white gown with a long train flowing behind.

But that was just a dream. It was something that would never come true. I wanted a nice wedding, but Bob (not his real name) had other ideas. He said he'd rather get married in a "Cracker Jacks box." So, we went to Yuma, Arizona and stood in line at a little chapel and said, "I do."

When we got back to Phoenix, I asked Bob if we could go to the Spaghetti Factory for dinner. It was fairly inexpensive, but still a popular place to eat. Besides, we had our marriage to celebrate.

However, Bob had other plans. He said we couldn't afford to eat out. He planned to celebrate our marriage by having frozen TV dinners on our wedding night.

I shouldn't have given in so easily. It was my wedding day too, and I didn't think it was too much to ask to have a nice meal on my wedding day. Although I was upset, I tried hard to just let it go and not let it spoil my wedding day.

I now believe that was the beginning of Bob controlling me.

We had dated for 2 years and I had never seen Bob get upset or behave in a jealous manner. We did not live together prior to our marriage, but just 2 weeks after we got married I realized that Bob had anger issues.

He was upset after I said hello to a gentleman at the pool at our apartment complex. Once we entered the apartment he started to yell at me, so I went into my purse and picked up the keys to my car. I wanted to leave long enough for Bob to calm down. He proceeded to push me inside of a closet and held his foot against the door so that I couldn't get out. After a few minutes I gave up trying to get out and sat down on the floor crying. I was in there for what seemed to be hours, but was probably more like 30 minutes. He later told me that he was sorry and that he was afraid I was going to leave him for good. In my mind I just accepted his apology, thinking that he would never do something like that again.

That was the first time that I witnessed Bob's insecurities and jealousy, but it certainly was not the last time.

As time went by many more incidents occurred. Bob ripped clothes off of me several times out of anger. He destroyed my record albums, broke dishes, and went into other violent rages. He once spit in my face while my sister Brenda was visiting from Ohio. He physically abused me by slapping me across my face on numerous occasions. He would defend his actions by telling me, "I don't hit you. I just slap you." I think in his mind he actually thought that he was doing me a favor by just slapping me and splitting my lip open, instead of punching me with his fist.

One incident that occurred will always stand out in my mind:

There was a time when we took our pug puppy, Goliath, to the park. We were enjoying the day when I said something that upset Bob. In an instant he picked up the puppy and then slammed him to the ground. I was absolutely shocked. How could this grown man hurt this innocent little puppy over something that I said? Fortunately Goliath survived, but this incident is etched in my mind forever.

After that incident occurred I was seriously thinking about divorcing Bob.

I always knew my parents would take me back with open arms, but I let my pride get in the way. I wanted to prove to my parents, as well as myself, that I could make it without their support. I didn't learn until later in life that I shouldn't let anything get in the way of using the support system available to me.

There were several reasons why I stayed in a physical and mentally abusive relationship. Even though I was independent prior to my marriage, I allowed myself to be beaten down, which in turn left me with low self-esteem. I was afraid to make decisions.

Being molested at such a young age and having been overweight had a profound impact on my life. My bad decisions led me down a dangerous path and many years of abuse.

Having done what many young women do in a troubled marriage, I got pregnant. I honestly believed that things would improve in our marriage; however, things only got worse. Now I had a child involved in my problems, a child that witnessed everything. My husband would hit me over the silliest things. But after each incident, he would apologize and swear to me that he would never do it again. I wanted to believe him, I wanted to think it would be the last time, but there was always a next time.

After my second son was born, I decided to do something about my weight, so I joined Weight Watchers. It was a program that I knew had many success stories, and I felt as though I could be successful as well.

After nine months I lost 60 pounds. I looked good and felt good about myself for the first time in my life. I thought my husband would be proud of me, but instead, it was as if I had taken Bob's security blanket away from him. With me being heavy, he thought that no one would ever look at me or pay any attention and that I would never be able to leave him. When I lost the weight he became more and more insecure. He became even more possessive and the violence occurred more often.

While I was married to Bob, we would take yearly vacations to Ohio. Typically, we would go our separate ways in Ohio. He would visit his family in Toledo and I would visit my family in Freedom. Our hometowns were at opposite ends of the state, so we felt that this worked best.

This particular year, 1985, I was staying with my sister when I received a call from an old high school friend. He asked if he could come by and visit, and of course, I said yes. When he arrived he was riding a motorcycle. After a warm greeting, he asked if I wanted to take a ride on his bike. I promptly said, "Yes." It wasn't everyday that I had an opportunity to ride a motorcycle. This would be an adventure.

He decided that we would go to Nelson Ledges State Park, which was about 10 miles from my sister's house. Once there, we started to hike into the ledges. We were about one mile into the hike when we came to a ravine. During our hike, my friend was hiking ahead of me, so by the time I reached the ravine my friend had already made the decision to jump. He jumped over a 100-foot-deep ravine, from one ledge, to a lower ledge.

Once I got to the ravine I had a choice. I either made the jump, or I would have to turn around and hike back to where we started from. My friend convinced me that it was an easy jump and that I would be fine. Since I didn't want to hike back alone, I decided to make the jump.

I got back and took off running toward the ravine. When I jumped, I was scared and I stiffened my leg and didn't bend at the knee. When I landed I heard a loud pop and then I felt excruciating pain. My leg was bent and I couldn't straighten it out. I tried to stand up but was unable to do so. My friend rushed to me and tried to help me up. But again, I was in so much pain that I couldn't even tolerate him touching me.

Every ounce of me was hurting and I didn't know what to do to ease the pain.

Unfortunately, this occurred prior to the cell phone era, so my friend and I were strategizing about what we should do to get me out of the ledges. About that time we saw a man and his young son approaching us. He asked if we needed help, we asked him to call for help when he got to the bottom of the ledges and he agreed to do so.

Thankfully help arrived within the hour. The paramedics brought a board, which they placed me on for the trip out of the ledges. When we got to the bottom, my friend asked if I wanted him to go to the hospital and I replied, "No!" I was angry with him for encouraging me to make the jump. For a long time I blamed him, but later I realized that I had no one to blame but myself. It was a decision that I would have to live with for the rest of my life. Making that jump caused me to have ongoing knee issues. By my living in Arizona and he in Ohio, we have never had the opportunity to speak about the incident.

The ambulance ride seemed to last forever, but finally we made it to the hospital. Once there I had a CAT scan to assess the damage. When the doctor came in to discuss my injuries, he stood at the foot of my bed. Unbeknownst to me, he had his hands on my toes, and all of a sudden he pulled my foot towards him very quickly as he attempted to straighten my leg. I let out a blood curdling scream that could be heard out in the waiting room. Later, my sister Brenda who was in the waiting room, told me she could hear me screaming.

The doctor explained that I had broken a bone in my knee, which split my tibia 10 centimeters. He said that I would require surgery the following morning. One bad decision cost me 10 days in the hospital and months of agonizing rehabilitation.

Fortunately, Bob was staying with his family in Toledo when the accident occurred. I had to come up with a story to tell Bob so that he didn't know that I was alone with a male friend. I feared what he would do to me if he ever found out. He certainly wouldn't understand that it was just an innocent hike through the ledges. So I told him that I went to the ledges with some friends from high school. Thankfully, he never questioned my story.

After returning from our trip we entered into marriage counseling, which helped temporarily. We stayed in counseling for approximately seven years, off and on. I know that is a very long time, but I just couldn't seem to get the courage to leave Bob until much later.

We both worked at the same manufacturing facility and part of the time we worked side by side. When he was around I felt like I had to wear blinders so that I didn't make eye contact with any males. If any male would say hello to me I would pay for it later. To this day, I cannot believe that my self esteem was so low that I would tolerate being treated that way.

The Christmas after I had broken my leg, Bob and I were home on Christmas vacation. Bob was lifting weights in the garage and I was watching the Sally Jesse Raphael show. The show was about multiple personalities, which I found interesting. I went out to the garage to tell Bob about the show and he said, "I don't have time for that and neither do you!" I was so upset at his comment, that I replied, "I'll watch it if I want to!"

Well, that was the wrong thing to say. Bob threw the bar bells across the garage and ran toward me. When he caught me he started to choke me. Our youngest son Daniel, who was 7 years old at the time, was there and begging his dad to stop, which he finally did. I felt lucky that Daniel was there and often wondered if he hadn't been, would Bob have choked me to death. Thankfully, I'll never know.

Bob's parents would come to Arizona and stay with us in our home for several months each year. They wanted to avoid the bad winters that residents in Ohio experience. One year, while they were staying with us, Bob had a 10k to run in Scottsdale. The boys and I always went to the runs so that we could cheer him on. Bob's parents opted to stay at home.

Leaving the Small Town

After the race was over, we got into the car and headed home. We came to a red light when I happened to glance at the car next to us. Instantly Bob accused me of looking at the guy in the car, and he back-handed me across the face. The boys started to cry, as they begged their dad to stop. When we got on the freeway he started to drive erratically and at a very high rate of speed. All I could think was that Bob was going to intentionally drive into the wall which separated the north and south bound traffic. I was afraid he was going to kill us all. Fortunately that didn't happen.

Once we got home, I went straight to my bedroom. I was so upset with Bob I could have just screamed! I certainly didn't want his parents to know what had just happened. For some crazy reason I felt embarrassed by his actions and didn't want anyone to know what was happening to me.

That was the day I knew it was over. I wasn't sure how I would support my children, but it was over. My job now was to protect my children and keep them safe. After my in-laws left to go back to Ohio I filed for divorce. I finally knew I had no other choice since this had gone on for 13 years and there was no end in sight.

After the freeway incident, dear friends of mine, Dan and Reatha Montoya, gave me the greatest gift I could imagine. They told me that if I wanted to leave Bob that they would help support me financially if I ever needed help. That was exactly what I needed to hear, I now had a safety net. I was very grateful to them for their offer. Even though I never needed their help, I always knew it was there for me if I needed it.

One year after our divorce, Bob came over to my house to pick the boys up. I was in the backyard so the boys let Bob come into the house. The next day Bob dropped the boys off and headed back home. After he left, Daniel proceeded to tell me that while Bob was in the house, the day before, he was snooping around. He happened to come across a card that my boyfriend had given me. I couldn't believe that he had the nerve to snoop in my house. Did he forget we were divorced? After stewing for a few minutes, I called him and told him that I knew he had gone through my personal things. I told him that going forward, he wasn't allowed in my house ever again. After hearing that, he screamed into the phone that he was coming over and slammed the phone down on me.

When he arrived at the house he started screaming for me to let him in. I was scared beyond belief. I knew if I let him in, it would be bad. He proceeded to tell me he would break down the door if I didn't let him. My thought process was that I wouldn't have the money to replace the door, so I opened it up to this out of control crazy man.

Once he was in, he ran toward me. He knew I was running toward the phone so that I could call 911. I didn't make it.

Leaving the Small Town

He beat me to the phone and yanked the cord out of the wall. He then proceeded to throw me up against the wall. I knew that I was in trouble, so I yelled to my son, Mike, who was 9 years old at the time, to go to the neighbors and call the police. He ran to a payphone and realized he didn't have a quarter (not knowing he didn't need a quarter to call 911), so he ran the opposite direction, to a friend's house. He asked the friend's dad to call the police and let them know that his dad was hurting his mom.

In the meantime, Bob left my house and went home. The police brought my son home and asked me what happened. I told them that Bob threw me against a wall. I explained that we had been divorced for a year and I didn't want to put up with his abuse any longer. They called Bob and told him that he needed to come back to my house so they could talk to him. When he arrived at the house, he was arrested on a domestic violence assault charge. He spent the night in jail and ended up having to take anger management classes.

Looking back, I wish I had taken my boys and myself to a shelter so that they would not have to witness the constant abuse. We could have started our lives over much sooner than we did. The fear of the unknown, as well as my pride took over during that time in my life. I didn't believe in myself and for that I made very bad decisions. I really should have considered my children and the emotional pain that they were going through. I can only imagine how frightened they must have been to see their father abusing their mother. If I had to do it all over again, I would have left after being locked in the closet.

God saw fit to test me again and though I may have required some time in working it out, I believe I was able to finally make the right decision with the tools he provided me.

CHAPTER 4

Moving On

For the first year after my divorce, my life still wasn't easy. I had two kids to raise and not a whole lot of money to do so. I was now a single mother trying to make it on my own. My boys were 9 and 11 years old, they were into sports, so keeping them active wasn't a problem. I stayed very busy, going to football and baseball games. Sometimes I would split my time up between games. I would attend half of one, then travel to the other game. It was a challenge, but most of the time it worked out. I loved my boys and enjoyed watching them grow up.

Once my divorce was final, I began to date. At the time, I worked for AT&T at the manufacturing facility in Phoenix. The plant was very large. They employed 3,500 people. I was a secretary in the maintenance department where I met Nick (not his real name). In the beginning I wasn't the least bit attracted to him. In fact, it took him three times asking me out before I agreed to go out with him. Nick was very much a smooth talker. He could sell ice to Eskimos if he wanted.

We went dancing every week, sometimes twice a week. We loved to country dance, so we would go to a country bar called Tooley's in Phoenix. We went with a group of our friends from the cable plant. Tooley's always had a live band so it was fun to go and listen to the various talent that they would attract. I was having the time of my life which was something I hadn't experienced before. Bob and I had never gone out, so this was a whole new life for me, and I liked it.

Nick made it clear from the beginning that he wasn't fond of kids, however I continued to date him. Besides, my boys had a father so it really shouldn't make that much difference, or so I thought. Nick had a problem with alcohol, the more he drank, the more he picked on my boys. So after three years I broke up with him.

We had been broken up for several months when Nick called and asked me to have lunch with him and I agreed. While having lunch, Nick said to me, "You are going to marry me." And I promptly replied, "No, I'm not." We went back and forth several times until I reminded Nick of his ill feelings for my boys. Nick tried to convince me that he had changed. God knows I wanted to believe him. He said we would take vacations, as well as other things together, as a family.

After taking into consideration all of the promises Nick made, I agreed to marry him. All I wanted was to be loved and cared about and I felt that Nick could give me that. Besides, he didn't abuse me like Bob did, so how bad could it be? All of my friends tried to talk me out of marrying Nick, but I didn't listen. I thought I knew better and that we could make it work. I wanted to be married and live happily ever after.

One thing before our marriage that did concern me was the fact that Nick drank alcohol frequently. He wasn't just a social drinker. He drank to get drunk just about every day of the week. But again, I thought he was about to make some major changes and I hoped drinking would be one of them.

Little did I know, my problems were just beginning.

Nick continued to drink and the more he drank the more belligerent he got.

In fact, after we were married all the promises he made went by the wayside. He continued to treat my boys badly. He wasn't physically abusive but rather verbally abusive. He did most things behind my back, but I always found out. It got so bad that my boys decided to move in with their dad. So in the end Nick got what he wanted, he got my kids to move out.

CHAPTER 5

Devastating News

Two years into our marriage I received a phone call from my ex-husband. He said that he was taking our son Daniel, who was only 15 years old at the time, to the doctor because he had a medical issue. I was at work so I asked my ex-husband to keep me informed. The next call I received was letting me know that Daniel's doctor was sending him to the emergency room. I immediately notified my manager that I needed to leave work. Nick and I carpooled together so we only had one car at work. I didn't care, I jumped in the car and headed to the hospital.

As I raced to the hospital, my heart was pounding. All I could think of was that he might need surgery. I didn't know what to think. As I got into the emergency room, I found

Daniel with my ex-husband being checked in. Daniel seemed to be in so much pain. He was doubled over the entire time.

Daniel was taken for an MRI while my ex-husband and I waited. We could hear the doctor yelling at our son, "Why didn't you tell someone? Why did you wait so long?" When the doctor emerged from behind the curtain where Daniel was, I asked "What is wrong with him?" He replied, "He has cancer and a one pound tumor has grown into his abdomen." The doctor sounded extremely upset as he shared with us that it was the worst case he had ever seen.

After receiving the news that Daniel had cancer, I got sick, feeling like I was going to faint. My head was spinning out of control as a million negative thoughts ran through me. I grabbed a chair, sitting down before I collapsed.

When I asked the doctor if my son was going to live, he said he didn't know. He said that he would need surgery immediately, so he was going to send Daniel back to the ER to be prepped. For the first time in many years, my ex-husband and I hugged each other as we cried together.

The doctor told me that I was welcome to sit in his office until I could compose myself. I took him up on his offer and began to make phone calls. The first call that I made was to Nick. I told him that I needed him to come to the hospital because Daniel had just been diagnosed with cancer. The next call I made was to my mom and dad. They were in shock as well. They said that they would be on their way to the hospital and would be there as soon as possible.

As I got into the elevator to visit Daniel, I tried to stay calm. I told myself that I had to be strong for Daniel. I knew I couldn't cry in front of him. What would I say to him? How would he react to the news? During my adult life I relied on my faith to get me through situations that were out of my control, so if there ever was a time that I prayed, I did then.

When I got into the room where Daniel was being prepped, I ran to him and threw my arms around him. I told him that I loved him and that he was going to be okay.

He had his baseball cap pulled down over his eyes, in an effort to hide his tears. He lifted up his cap, looked me in the eye, and asked me if he was going to die. I promptly replied, "No!"

He asked, "What percentage are they giving me to live?" I sternly answered that it didn't matter if they gave him a 1% chance of survival, I wouldn't accept anything less of him than to survive. My answers seemed to help, not only him, but me as well.

Nick had a friend drive him to the hospital since I had taken our car. When he finally showed up at the hospital he had the ER nurse come and get me. I fell into his arms bursting into tears, telling him I was afraid that Daniel was not going to make it.

He consoled me for about a minute and then he checked his watch and then abruptly said, "Babe, I've gotta go, Joe (his boss) has an important meeting in about 30 minutes."

I asked, "You're leaving me here to deal with this by myself?"

He replied, "Yes, I really have to go."

So off he went, taking our car with him. He left without ever seeing Daniel. I was absolutely stunned that this man could be so heartless.

How could my husband, the man who supposedly loved me, just walk out on me during the worst day of my life? How could this man be so cold, not only to me, but Daniel as well? Who was this man? Could he have always been this heartless?

I knew at that moment, when Nick left, that my marriage to him was over. I just had to wait until Daniel got through battling his cancer.

If not for my parents and my ex-husband I would have been totally alone at the hospital. My parents stayed there and comforted me throughout the day. My sister, Brenda, now lived in Omaha, Nebraska, so she was unable to be with

Devastating News

me. My parents and my sister were the only people that I could really count on.

I stayed at the hospital until Daniel came out of recovery, which was about 10 o'clock that evening. My ex-husband and I were the only ones left at the hospital by this time. Since Nick had taken our car when he left, I had to ask my ex-husband for a ride home. Yes, that's right, my ex-husband, Bob, took me home.

When I got home I noticed that Nick was drunk, which really didn't surprise me. He asked me how Daniel was doing and I said, "Not good" and I burst into tears. Nick responded by yelling, "Stop your God damn crying." I probably shouldn't have been but I was absolutely shocked at his behavior... I didn't know this man anymore and maybe I never did. My son's situation was the worst possible experience to have to go through and I felt so alone, hurting like never before.

CHAPTER 6

Living With Cancer

Daniel was only 15 years old and had his whole life ahead of him. I admit to being in shock for some time, how could this be happening to him? He was my baby. I felt such a huge cloud over my head not knowing if I was going to bury my son or not. The feeling of despair haunted me for days. How could I bring myself out of this feeling of dread? How could I ever feel happy again? If ever I needed to be strong, it was now.

Daniel spent 10 days in the hospital during which time he had his first round of chemotherapy. On day four, Daniel's diagnoses came back. With the type of cancer that Daniel had, he was given a 65% chance of survival. I was ecstatic. It could have been so much worse.

Daniel did his best to stay positive and upbeat. He missed most of his Sophomore year in high school. Most days he was sick from the chemo. When he did go to school, he took only one class and that was art. We knew that the year would pretty much be a wash, but we wanted him to go to school mainly for the socialization and to keep his mind occupied.

Daniel came home from school one day and said that a boy in his class had committed suicide by shooting himself in the head. He said, "Mom, I don't understand why he would do something like that, being healthy and all. Here I am fighting for my life and this kid just takes his own life."

I knew from this conversation that my son had just been taught a valuable lesson in life, to cherish life and never take it for granted. We need to take every day and appreciate the things we have and live life to the fullest. We have to remember that everything is temporary, the good times in life as well as the bad. Perhaps this is why God sent us this trial, for us to learn and expand our strength for life.

My parents were wintering in Arizona, so they helped me by transporting Daniel to and from his chemo treatments. They were such a huge help, as I had to work during this time. They would take him once a week for his chemo treatment. These treatments were fairly quick, but every third week he would have to spend the day hooked up to an IV which dispersed chemo into Daniel's body.

Once my parents headed back to Ohio in the spring, I reached out to the Cancer Society for help with transportation. Although Nick worked the night shift and could have helped out, I knew I couldn't rely on him.

The Cancer Society has volunteers that will transport cancer patients in need. At this time in my life, I needed them now urgently as I had to work and couldn't take time off from work. They assigned an elderly couple to transport Daniel. They were retired school teachers. It was amazing that they gave of their time to such a wonderful organization. I couldn't have done it without them.

One day Daniel relayed to me that when the volunteers arrived to pick him up, Nick answered the door and yelled to Daniel that his ride was here. Having had a brand new Ford F150 sitting in the driveway, and a "healthy" Nick answer the door was quite embarrassing. I'm sure that the volunteers must have wondered why Nick couldn't transport Daniel.

As the year went on, Daniel became sicker and sicker with each chemo treatment he received. He had me shave his head soon after he started the chemo treatments because his hair was falling out by the handful. I'll never forget what he said to me as I was shaving his head. He said, "It's really going to suck if I die after going through all of this." I quickly made an excuse to leave the room because I couldn't hold back the tears. My heart ached for him. What a horrible thing for my son to go through at such a young age.

It was a very tough year, as I felt compelled to let Daniel do most of what he wanted to do. As time went on, I found Daniel pushing life to the limit. He was staying out past curfew and ignoring everything I asked him to do. Knowing what he was going through made it very difficult to punish him. I felt that he was living on the edge because he didn't know if he was going to survive this awful thing called "cancer."

As the one year mark approached, Daniel was going in for his last and final chemo treatment. The doctor wanted Daniel to go into the hospital as his treatments were taking a toll on him, but he refused to go. So the doctor agreed to let him stay at home with one exception.

We had to have a nurse come to our home and have an IV hooked up to Daniel. She instructed me on how to administer the anti-vomiting medication as part of getting me familiar with all that would happen that night. After she left it was up to me to take care of Daniel, which frightened me. I had absolutely no medical experience and now I was suppose to take care of my son's medical needs.

As the night went on, Daniel became sicker by the minute. I was beginning to think that we made a big mistake by not having him go to the hospital for his treatment. At one point he said he felt as though he was dying inside. He was vomiting every 30 to 40 minutes, so by five o'clock in the morning I placed a call to his doctor. The doctor told me to take him to the hospital immediately.

Daniel wasn't able to walk, so I asked Nick to carry him to the car for me, which he did. That was the one and only thing that Nick did to help me during the past year. While we were on the freeway, driving to the hospital, Daniel sat with a bucket on his lap. He was throwing up the entire way to the hospital. He asked me not to get too close to other cars because he didn't want anyone to see him. I felt helpless!

By the time we got to the hospital, I was an emotional wreck. They put Daniel in a room and hooked up a new IV, which actually started to control the vomiting. I stood outside his room and began to cry uncontrollably.

A nurse spotted me and walked over and began to comfort me. I told her that I wished I could take his place. I wished it were me enduring his pain. She told me she understood how I felt and it was natural for me to feel this way. She convinced me to go home and get some sleep since I had been up all night. She assured me that Daniel would be fine and that I could come back later in the day and pick him up which I did.

Three months later, I took Daniel in for an MRI to see if the cancer was in remission.

The Spirit Within Me

Several days later we got the news that we were praying for. Daniel was cancer free!

We were ecstatic.

We could finally breathe easy. No more chemo treatments and best of all no more pain and suffering.

Daniel could finally live his life like a normal 16-year-old.

We had survived our trial, the lesson for both Daniel and me on perseverance against all odds and to not lose faith in each other.

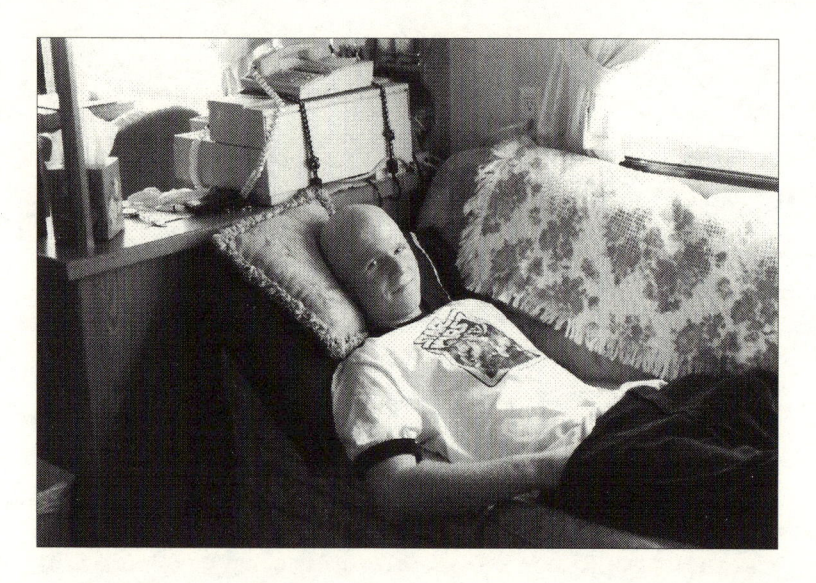

CHAPTER 7

Staying True

Staying true to the promise I made to myself, I divorced Nick.

He was never a loving, caring, or supportive husband, especially during the past year. He had belittled my boys, as well as me, long enough. His drinking continued to the point that I couldn't take it any more.

I wished I had listened to my friends. As it turned out they were right. They were able to see things that I couldn't. I wanted to believe in Nick, but instead he proved my friends right.

The end result was that I lost four years of my life to an abusing alcoholic.

One week after I moved out of our house, I went by Nick's house to pick up the last of my belongings. While I was there, Nick told me that he went to a priest and asked for advice on how to get through the divorce. He claimed that the priest suggested that he give it one more try. While he was telling me this, he began to cry and pleaded with me to move back home.

Since I had been through this with him before, I could see right through the crocodile tears. I knew from past history, he couldn't be trusted. The old cliché, "Fool me once, shame on you, fool me twice, shame on me," was screaming out at me loud and clear.

Before I left, my son Mike got back at Nick in his own way. He knew that Nick was going out that night, so he filled his boots up with shaving cream. While I was there, Nick put his boots on; he was so drunk that he was oblivious to the fact that Mike had messed with them. After he left, Mike and I laughed until we cried. I told him weeks later about what Mike did and he got very angry. However, I think he knew he had it coming.

As it turned out, Nick was fine without me. Two weeks after I moved out he had moved another woman into our house. Not surprising, he met her in a bar. She had a 16-year-old daughter who moved into our house as well.

This lady was from a very rough part of town and I didn't trust her. I had Nick's name removed from my life insurance policy effective immediately. I didn't want to take any chances prior to our divorce being finalized.

He thought I was being silly, but I really didn't know what she might do.

CHAPTER 8

Back to School

Here I was, a 41-year-old, twice divorced single woman. Both of my son's, by then 18 and 20 years old, had moved out. I was truly on my own.

After my divorce from Nick, I decided to go back to school after much coaxing from my mother. She was right. With the economy in a down slide, I needed a degree in order to keep my job. So while working, I went to school full time. It was one of the most intimidating things I ever did, especially since I had been out of school for about 25 years.

On my first day of school, my dad packed a lunch for me as if I were headed off to kindergarten for the first time. I think he liked the idea of taking care of his "little" girl. I thanked my dad and headed out the door. My parents were staying with me during the winter time and I think they were re-living the days when I was younger. It was a loving and sweet thing to experience.

Going back to school really turned out to be a blessing; I made a lot of new friends along the way. We worked in study groups and developed very close friendships over the years. After three years, I graduated with a Bachelor of Science in Business Management.

Just before I graduated I started to date again. A dear friend of mine, Dodds Tyler, wanted to introduce me to a friend of his, named Rod, who was also his coworker. I agreed to meet him for dinner on a blind date. He was a police officer, so I trusted him to pick me up at my house.

I went into this date with no expectations, so I was pleasantly surprised when I answered the door.

He was tall, dark and very handsome. He had done his homework and found out that I liked seafood. So he took me to a very nice seafood restaurant. We enjoyed a scrumptious dinner of my favorite, scallops and lobster, while getting to know each other.

I told him that I had two adult sons, Mike and Daniel. He told me that he had an adult son named Paul and an adult daughter named Jennifer.

He also nervously told me that he has been divorced twice. I was so relieved, it made it so much easier for me to tell him that I was also divorced twice. After dropping me off at my house, we hugged each other goodnight.

The very next day Rod called me and asked me out on a second date and I happily agreed to go out with him. I really wanted to get to know this guy since we had so much in common. He took me bowling on our second date and we had a great time laughing and joking with each other. I think he was getting a little nervous because I came close to beating him. This time, at the drop off at my house, he kissed me goodnight.

We seemed to get along so well, but I was leery of any relationship.

I had two divorces behind me. I had no intentions of ever marrying again. However, after dating for only three months we moved in together. I know what you are all thinking: that crazy woman, what was she thinking. Somehow, I knew it was right, I knew Rod was good for me... we just clicked.

After we were together for ten months Rod convinced me to go back to school and obtain a Master's degree. I thought long and hard, but in the end I knew it was for the best. Besides, my tuition was covered through my employer, so I had everything to gain.

The Spirit Within Me

So here I was, in my mid-forties, no kids living with me, headed back to school. I had the study routine down, so I knew it would be a little easier this time around. Rod worked a lot of overtime on his job, so it was a good time for me to return to school. It was difficult, but we seemed to always have time to do things together. We took a lot of weekend trips, as well as several cruises.

Life was finally turning around for me. It was awesome.

After two years I graduated with a Master of Arts in Organizational Management. That was a very proud day, since I had never considered going to college as a young adult.

Here I was, the girl who didn't think she was smart enough to go to college, with a Master's degree. I was finally starting to believe in myself.

My graduation came at a great time as Rod's overtime was winding down. Now we could look forward to both of our retirements, which was about nine years off.

CHAPTER 9

The Proposal

Christmas in 2004 was a very special time.

My entire family came to Arizona to spend the holidays with us. I carried on the tradition that my dad started and had a Christmas Eve party.

After dinner we all opened gifts. I noticed that Rod became very antsy. I was oblivious to what was happening until Rod got down on one knee. He pulled a ring out of his pocket, and asked me to marry him. I was in shock, I had had no idea this was coming.

Rod said, "Well?" and I realized I hadn't given him an answer.

So I quickly responded with, "Yes I'll marry you!"

The Spirit Within Me

I agreed to get married again. But this time was different; I knew that this was right. It was really right. Besides, Rod and I had been together for four years, and there hadn't been any red flags.

Now I had a wedding to plan. We wanted to have a simple wedding with all of our friends and relatives. Nothing fancy, just nice. So on November 5th, 2005, we got married. My sister Brenda was my matron of honor and Rod's son Paul was his best man.

Our reception was one big party. It was so wonderful to get everybody together to celebrate our marriage. And this time it was, "In sickness and in health, until death do us part!"

The Proposal

Over the next several years, Rod and I worked hard, the whole time looking forward to our retirement. We went on as many trips as possible. We enjoyed trips to Tennessee and Nebraska to visit my parents and sister, as well as taking several cruises.

Life was finally going in the right direction. I had the most wonderful husband, a beautiful home, and no stress in my life for the first time ever.

CHAPTER 10

Life Changing Event

Fast forward to December 2011. We were making plans to go to Tennessee to spend Christmas with my entire family.

We were going to be staying in a cabin which had five bedrooms. My mom and dad, my sister Brenda and her husband Rick, their son Jon, my brother Keith and his girlfriend, Paul (Rod's son) and his wife, Tiff, would all be staying in the cabin. It was certainly going to be a houseful which is just the way we liked it.

Rod and I flew to Tennessee on December 22nd. We arrived at the airport in Nashville and were greeted by my mom and dad. The plan was to stay the night at their house and head to the cabin in the morning. We loaded our luggage in the back of their truck and off we went to begin our holiday. Since my parents were getting up there in years, I tried to help them out whenever I could. I volunteered to drive my dad's truck back to their house as it was a long trip.

The next morning, we woke up excited. We were going to stop at the airport in Knoxville to pick up my nephew Jon on our way to the cabin. My sister Brenda and her husband, Rick, would be arriving later that day and since they were renting a car we wouldn't need to pick them up. My brother Keith and his girlfriend lived near my parents, so they would be coming in later that day. Rod's daughter Jennifer and her husband, Enan, and Enan's parents who were also renting a separate cabin just down from ours, would also be in that day; they were coming from South Carolina and Maryland. Finally, Rod's son Paul and his wife, Tiff, would be arriving on Christmas Eve. They were coming from Phoenix, Arizona. A lot of people, traveling from all over the country, coming together for the holidays.

That evening we all partied at our cabin; everyone was in such a festive mood. We were enjoying cocktails, telling stories and laughing until we cried. That's how my family was. We knew how to live and be happy no matter how good or bad things are. This was truly going to be the best Christmas ever.

CHAPTER 11

The Uncertainty

The next morning when I woke up and I went to the kitchen, my dad was already in there. I sat down with him and we started to chitchat for a while. Everyone else started to rise and we all congregated in the kitchen.

Brenda, her son Jon and I went into her bedroom, sat on the bed and began to reminisce. It was so wonderful to be with my sister again. I miss her so much whenever we are apart. To have her there in my presence was truly fulfilling.

We behaved as children do, laughing and carrying on, just being silly.

All of a sudden I felt a terrible pain in my chest. I grabbed Brenda's hands and told her that I thought I was having a heart attack. Brenda yelled for Rod. Rod promptly entered the room and Brenda left to go call 911.

I began to hyperventilate as the pain increased. I told Brenda not to let my parents in the room as I didn't want to upset them. My dad ignored my request and came in anyway. He brought an aspirin with him and had me take it.

When the paramedics arrived they ran some tests, which showed that I wasn't having a heart attack. They asked me if I still wanted to go to the hospital. I said, "Yes," and they loaded me onto a gurney and headed to a waiting ambulance.

At the hospital the doctors ran several tests. The first test was blood work, checking my enzymes, which showed no heart attack. The next test was a treadmill test which I passed. Lastly, they did a dye test and that lit up like a Christmas tree.

They finally diagnosed my condition: I was having an aortic dissection. Basically, in layman's terms, my aorta which is attached to the heart, was shredding from the top down and the bottom up.

The hospital that I was at didn't have the ability to perform the surgery that was required. So within minutes, I was being taken to a waiting helicopter. I told Rod that I was scared and didn't want to die, I loved him and asked him to tell Mike and Daniel that I loved them too.

The Uncertainty

Rod later relayed to me that at that point all he knew was that whatever this aortic dissection was, it was serious. However, he didn't know just how serious it really was until later on that evening. He found out that less than 5% of patients with this condition survive.

I was being flown to Parkwest Medical Center where the surgery would be performed. Since Rod rode in the ambulance to the first hospital, he needed a ride to Parkwest Medical Center. He contacted Rick, my brother-in-law and filled him in on my condition. Brenda and Rick were at a grocery store when they got the news. Brenda was so shocked by the diagnosis, she dropped to her knees. Rick told her to get up and get ahold of herself. He told her that Rod was waiting for them to pick him up and take him to the hospital.

Rod, Rick and Brenda arrived at the hospital, only to be told that I was already in surgery. They were told that my surgery would last three to four hours. As hour five came they became very concerned. What could be taking so long?

After the sixth hour the doctor (Dr. Maggart) emerged to go over my condition. He started by drawing a picture of my heart and aorta. He began to rattle things off so quickly, telling my family I was lucky to be alive and how serious the situation was. He explained how my aorta started to shred from the top down and the bottom up. He also said that initially he thought that my aorta was the only problem I had, but once my chest was cracked open he found that a valve had torn off from my heart as well. That is why my surgery took as long as it did. The doctor also said that machines kept me alive for 24 minutes during part of the surgery. Then he also mentioned that I hadn't woken up yet and he didn't know why.

It was a lot of information for my family to process in such a short period of time.

By this time it was getting late, so they went back to the cabin to share the news with the rest of my family. Obviously, the Christmas Eve party was canceled. Everyone needed time to absorb what had just taken place.

I had gone to the gym as often as possible, ran on a treadmill and ate as healthily as I could. So why did this happen to me? What had I done to bring on this horrific incident?

The doctor said that it was brought on by high blood pressure or stress. I had high blood pressure, but it was controlled with medication. As for stress, while my early years had been through many crazy trials, I hadn't been under any stress since I met Rod. So, could it have been because I was under so much stress prior to Rod and it finally caught up to me?

Maybe it was just God's will to test me again and see how strong I had actually become.

CHAPTER 12

My Faith

Growing up in Ohio as a little girl, I attended the local church religiously. However, as I grew older I found that while I kept my faith in God, I lost my faith in man. It seemed to me that organized religion was just interested in the almighty dollar.

After moving to Arizona, I attended several Lutheran churches. They provided us with numbered envelopes so they could keep track of how much money we were giving each week. At the end of each quarter the church would send out a statement letting you know if you were on track with your pledge, or how far behind you were. In my case, I was always behind. Feeling guilty about being behind on pledges just depressed me and it wasn't worth it anymore, so I just stopped going to church. Besides, the sermon always seemed to be focused on the offerings and how important it was to make good on your pledge.

Even though I questioned the organized churches, I still believed in God and remained very spiritual. I tried to always be good to others and lived my life to the best that I knew how. I knew that I would go to heaven because I was a good person and lived a good clean life.

After my health crisis, over the next several days, my family quickly got the word out to friends, coworkers and other family members, and asked that they pray for me. Before my family knew it, there were prayer chains all around the country, as well as around the world. My sister worked with people in Ireland, China, Singapore, Korea, Australia and India. They were all praying for my survival.

The next morning, everyone woke to a dark cloud over their heads, Christmas morning and no one felt like celebrating. Instead, everyone got ready and headed to the hospital. Once there they had to go back two at a time. Those were the rules in the ICU (intensive care unit).

Rod said that when he entered my room, I was laying there as if I was peacefully sleeping. Hard to tell that I was actually fighting for my life. While there, my hands and legs began to twitch and everyone got very excited, thinking I was about to wake up. However, the nurse told them that I was actually having seizures.

CHAPTER 13

The Journal

Brenda came up with the idea of keeping a journal. That way they would be able to remember everything that was happening during a time that they were all so overwhelmed.

The following are journal entries that were made by Rod and my family. My sister Brenda sent out email updates, which I have included as well.

Rod 12/24/11

Today is Christmas Eve day. Paul and Tiff (son and daughter-law) will be arriving today. We are going to have a great vacation with everybody. It's around nine o'clock, or so, and as usual, I'm in the kitchen preparing about four different things for dinner tonight.

All of a sudden Brenda yelled that something was wrong with Pam and she needed me in the back bedroom. I went back there and Pam was laying on her back on the bed, holding her chest and hyperventilating. She looked at me and said "call 911, I think I'm having a heart attack". I honestly thought that Pam was having some sort of anxiety attack. Some of the symptoms are the same, such as tightness of the chest, trouble breathing, etc. I tried to calm Pam down, which helped a little. Larry (dad) gave Pam an aspirin to thin her blood. The paramedics got there pretty quick. They loaded her up and I went with her to the Medical Center. When we got there, the doctor started out with a series of blood tests. The results were negative for a heart attack. Next, they did a stress test and the results again were negative. She said she had pain in her chest still, but I was feeling pretty sure after the first two tests that this still was just going to be an anxiety attack. The doctor said that they had one more test to perform, which was a dye test. He came back a few minutes later, and my whole life changed.

Before I knew it, the helicopter guys were in her room, putting her onto a gurney. She looked at me and said, "I don't want to die." That broke my heart when she said that. I tried to reassure her by saying that they would take good care of her and fix her up and that I would never let her die. Pam asked me to tell Mike and Daniel that she loved them.

The Journal

Then Pam said to me from her gurney, "I always thought this would be you." The last thing that Pam said to me before they took her to the helicopter was "I love you." I touched my heart and I said, "I love you too."

I have never felt so helpless before, not being able to do anything to help her. I just watched as the helicopter took off. I am hoping that nothing goes wrong during surgery. I don't know what I would do without Pam. She is the love of my life. We have so many things to look forward to. Paul and Tiff's new baby, Rick and Brenda moving to Arizona, retirement. My God we have so many good things coming up. Come on baby please don't leave me... Please!

We were allowed to see her after her surgery. Oh my God, she had a respirator in her mouth, and so many IVs going into her arms. She looked like she had about 20 different IV bags going into her. We saw the scar down the center of her chest. I was just stunned. I'm just looking at her and thinking what the hell just happened? We were partying, singing, dancing, having a great time one minute, and the next minute this!

Not Pam. She's too young, too healthy, too full of life. She's the leader of the Conga line, the social butterfly... This just could not be happening!!! I feel like a 1,000 pound weight has been dropped on my heart. C'mon Pam, enough fooling around. Wake up baby...Please wake up.

I just feel like I am in a bad nightmare, and I just want to wake up and have you look at me, and tell me to lay on my stomach because I was snoring. But this is real, and there is nothing I can do to help you. I'm surrounded by family, and the one person I love most in this world isn't by my side. I miss you so much it hurts. You are breaking my heart Pam. Please wake up, please. I can't believe how much I miss you.

Brenda 12/25/11

I talked to Aunt Linda, she's very concerned for you. She cried with me on the phone. She is keeping Randy (cousin) and Claudia (cousin) updated. Linda told me to continue talking in your ear. I keep saying "Pami, it's time to wake up, please wake up. Open your eyes Pam." Everyone has been coming in and holding your hand and talking to you. We all miss you! We're not complete without you. I love you sissy.

Rod 12/25/11

We are all visiting you at the hospital. You're still not awake yet. That's not good. I brought a Santa hat in and put it on your little melon, and took a picture so you would know we're all thinking about you on Christmas day.

They gave me another knee to the nuts. They said that they needed to do a CT scan, an E.K.G, and a MRI on your brain, to see why you aren't waking up. They said that you'd be in and out of your room for the rest of the day so we decided to go back to the cabin and celebrate Christmas day, since that is what you would want.

Everyone was at the cabin, everyone but my baby! I gave a toast, which was adopted by a famous philosopher, it went, "Here's to Pam she's going to heal the more we pray the better she will feel. Here's to you baby" Then I asked everyone to hold hands and say a silent prayer for you. I know, I know, I don't pray. But you asked me to save it for when I really needed it. Well baby I need it, I need you!

Damn you woman for making me feel this way about you! I'm not a big fan of the emotions. Well it's off to bed for another night of 3-4 hours of sleep. I miss you so much!

Brenda 12/26/11

Waiting for E.K.G. testing. Everyone is at the hospital to see you Pam. We noticed your thumb moving while Tiff was holding your hand. We love you Pam, and are eagerly waiting for you to wake up.

Paul (step son) 12/26/11

Still in complete shock Pam. When we landed at the airport, Tiff and I were burning out in circles in the parking lot not knowing where we were going after getting the news.

We were at the hospital during your surgery. Minutes seemed like hours. Lots of tears, love, and prayers going out for you Pam. After 6 hours of surgery, you toughed it out. What a relief!

The doctors have you sedated, and we are waiting for you to wake up. Christmas night we are having some drinks for our Pam. Tiff and I surprised everybody with the news that she is pregnant. Dad asked everybody to pray for you before eating dinner... followed by more tears.

Rick (brother-in-law) 12/26/11

Emotional roller coaster. Just received news of having definite seizures in the brain. An MRI has been ordered for tomorrow. Barbara the nurse strongly indicated we need to take baby steps. Basically we need to wait until the results of the MRI are reviewed. The MRI is a very important process because of what it will reveal. It could take a couple of days for the results.

Rod 12/26/11

Today is Jenn's (daughter) birthday. She said that she doesn't mind that I am visiting you at the hospital. I told her that I'd try to do something with her tonight. During one of our visits, we finally got to talk to the neurologist. Here comes another kick in the nuts! He said that after looking at the CT scan, there was no signs of large trauma, or damage, but the E.K.G showed multiple seizures in the brain, and the MRI showed numerous mini strokes. I went numb.

All I could think of is Eric's (editor note: a police officer who had been in a horrific motorcycle accident) situation, when he survived his surgery, but didn't even recognize his wife. I don't know what I'd do if that happened with you. I pray that you come out of this the same person you were before, and that you know me, and still love me. We can deal with any physical problems: speech, walking, whatever, I just need you to be you. I just can't believe this is happening to you. You are too good of a person. It's just not right!

Paul, Tiff and Jon decided to go to the Texas Roundhouse after leaving the hospital, so they called and invited Brenda, Rick, and myself to join them. On the way there, Brenda finally lost it. She started screaming at God, saying how unfair it was, how you are such a good person, etc. She was pounding on the car seat and on her legs, yelling at the world. I felt the same way. I feel like I could put my fist through a wall right now. When we got to the restaurant, Rick stopped in the parking lot to let me out. Brenda was talking to me when the car behind us started to honk their horn. Brenda stuck her arm out the window, flipped the guy off and said f@#& you! Poor Breni, she loves you so much, we all do!

Brenda 12/27/11
8:30 A.M. Visit

Rick and I went in to see you, and they had you hooked up to these sticky patches all around your head, which was for the MRI. My favorite thing to do is to run my fingers through your hair. That was not the thing to do this morning! Nurse Barbara had to tell me not to touch your head. I found myself starting to touch your hair about four more times. I held, and rubbed your hand so that I wouldn't get into trouble with our favorite nurse, Ms Barbara. I love you and miss you Sis!

We just got home from visiting Pam. Nothing has changed... Keep waiting to hear some good news. Rod is cooking Mexican food. He just asked me to do him a favor and yell at him once in awhile, letting him know that he is preparing way too much food. He said that he misses Pam, as she would have already said that couple of times.

Rod 12/27/11

No change. This waiting is killing me. Finally, I got to talk to a neurologist today. I don't think my nuts can take anymore kicks, but here comes another one. He said that it looks like because of all of the strokes Pam will have brain damage. He said they won't know the extent of the damage until they get you to wake up, and they can't wake you up until they get the brain seizures under control. He said they will give you some heavy drugs and may have to put you in a medically induced coma. I don't care what the hell they do, just wake up... soon!

Brenda 12/28/11

My eyes are still swollen from all of the crying I have done since 12/24/11. It still feels like I am in a bad dream.

I so badly want to wake up and tell you my terrible dream. It just can't be true. It just can't be... my heart is so heavy, I feel so sad. I keep praying to God; I want him to give us a miracle. Please give us some good news today. I want so badly to have my Sissy back. I didn't know your heart could ache so much for someone.

Rick and I have to leave today to go home to Omaha. While we were at the airport we got a call from Rod, he had just visited with you. He informed me that you had several mini strokes. Not the news we wanted to hear. On the brighter side it was mini strokes, and not major. I'm looking for anything positive, I'm digging... This is a nightmare. I just want to wake up. I want the life that I knew prior to December 24th. I love you Sissy!

I want you to open your eyes and give us that big beautiful smile... I don't want you to feel any pain. Dad told me last night "I would trade places with her if I could. I think all of us would" You're the strength, the rock of our family. We always looked up to you. You were always the one to organize the family trips. You and Linda are planning Dad's 80th birthday party. I need for you to get better Sissy I want you there. I love you.

Rod 12/28/11

Absolutely no news about Pam. Maybe my nuts will heal today. The only thing hurting me now is my heart. Still crying like a little girl, can't help it, damn it.

Rod 12/29/11

No news with Pam. Still not awake. I heard that Dan and Mike are driving here to be with her. I was glad to hear that. It would mean the world to Pam to know that they cared enough to come. The doctors said that they will try to reduce the number of medications and see if the seizures stop. If they stop she has to go 48 hours with no more seizures, then they can slowly wake her up. The waiting is killing me. I just want to see her open her eyes. You always said that you wanted me to be more patient, well I don't like it. Not one bit!

Rick 12/30/11

As I am getting ready to take Brenda to the airport, I just can't quit thinking how unfair this is. As each day passes from when Pam went into the hospital, and the news of her condition keeps getting worse and worse. The reality of everything is unbelievable. It just isn't fair having so much in front of her, and knowing all of the positive things that were happening in her life. Damn it, wake up Pam!

Rod 12/30/11

Daniel, Amanda (Daniel's girlfriend), and Mike arrived. They got in late last night, and were exhausted. When everyone woke up in the morning, we all came to visit. You would have been very proud of your boys. They held up very well. That's not to say that they weren't devastated, just that they didn't fall apart.

By the way, I still haven't shaved yet. I told you I wouldn't shave until you yelled at me to do so. I have to have Breni to Pamitize me every once in awhile. She would tell me not to cook so much food, put some shoes on etc. It's not quite the same, but it helps. I especially like when she calls me an ass... Ahhh, fond memories... wake up baby, wake up.

Rod 12/31/11

Well, it's New Years Eve, and it means absolutely nothing to me because I can't spend it with Pam. I can't believe that I am surrounded by family that I love, and think the world of, but I feel so alone. Larry (editor note: dad) is cooking his traditional pork and sauerkraut for New Years Eve dinner. The whole family will be here tonight for dinner. We visited Pam early in the day and she just looks like she is sleeping. Come on baby just wake up, just open your eyes, let me know everything will be okay.

Daniel called from the hospital, and said that Pam had coughed two, or three times, and that the nurse said that it could be a sign that she was starting to wake up. They said that it looks like she was trying to open her eyes also. I try not to get too depressed, or too happy about any news because they said that this is going to be a long process with many ups and downs. It's so hard not to get my hopes up because I feel like all I have heard so far is bad news.

Larry heard the news and he finally lost it. Poor Larry was crying and crying and saying how happy he was. I had to give him a big hug. Everybody here was ecstatic. Mike, Dan, Amanda, Brenda and I decided that we are going back to the hospital now!!!

I was really hoping that I would see you with your eyes open when we got there, but no such luck. That was just another aching blow. I just want to see you open your eyes. C'mon Pam, it's New Years Eve! We need you to lead the party. The nurse, "Debbie Downer," as Dan calls her, said that it will be 24 to 48 hours before you'll probably be awake.

We drove home, ate some of Larry's delicious sauerkraut and went to bed. I won't be celebrating anything tonight. Not until I have you back. Happy New Years baby!

Brenda 12/31/11

Rod, mom and I drove in one car, while Mike, Dan, Amanda, and Keith were in another car. I just couldn't wait to see you! I just flew into Tennessee the evening of 12/30/11. I missed you since flying back to Omaha on 12/28/11. We got some really good news from the kids. They saw you trying to cough. The best news we've had in a week!

I decided to call your nurse, Andrew, and he told me that you opened your eyes for a moment. Rod was so excited, he said, "I'm going back to the hospital." So, we all piled into mom's car, and headed back. Nurse Jane, also known as "Debbie Downer," was on shift. She acted as if it was no big deal that you opened your eyes. Well, it was to us!

I want you to wake up; we miss you so much. You are such a wonderful, loving sister. I want you back... tomorrow is going to be a better day. I love you Sissy! Happy New Year!

Rod 01/01/12

It's New Years Day. Brenda, Larry, Jackie and I went to visit you. You still haven't opened your eyes for me. You just look like you are sleeping. Nurse Patty actually said some positive things. She said that the strokes in your head were like little polka dots, and they weren't spreading, or getting bigger. She also said that there were no new ones. I asked if the ones that were already there could be repaired by the brain. She said, "Yes, they can repair themselves, and sometimes affected areas re-route themselves." Nurse Patty said that it could still be 24 - 48 hours before you come around. It feels like I've heard 24 - 48 hours for a week now.

We drove home after our visit, and I made dinner. Daniel called from the hospital and said that you tried to open your eyes about 10 times. He also said that you were trying to lean forward, and you were coughing.

Brenda and I drove back for the last two visits of the night. The first visit was more of the same. You didn't move, you didn't open your eyes... nothing! I think you are messing with me woman! All I want is to see you open your eyes. C'mon baby, throw us a bone!

The last visit was the same as the first. No movement, nothing! Just as we are about to leave, for the night, you did it! You opened your peepers!!! It wasn't a lot, it wasn't long, but we were ecstatic. Finally, we have a glimmer of hope! C'mon baby, come back to us. You can do it. We'll be here as long as it takes.

Rod 01/02/12

During our visit, you opened your eyes a little wider, and it looked like you were trying to track us with your eyes. The nurse said that the neurologist was going to start reducing the anti seizure medication tomorrow. By doing that, it may make it easier for you to wake up. I'm hopeful that tomorrow will be a better day, and that you will be alert, and responsive.

As soon as you start being more responsive, they can take that damn respirator out. It kills me to see how much you hate that thing. Again... I feel so damn helpless. There is absolutely nothing I can do to help you, and when I see you in pain, I just want to scream. I just want you to start responding, then we'll be able to see what we'll need to work on. We can handle anything they throw at us. You are a tough, strong willed woman and I know you'll do everything you can to get back to where you were. And I will be with you every step of the way. I love you baby, keep fighting!

Rod 01/03/12

Baby it's cold outside. It snowed last night. I'm making soup and salad today. I've been doing a lot of cooking to take my mind off of your situation. The distraction helps for a little while, but then my mind goes right back to you. I miss your laugh. I miss making you laugh and then you calling me an ass. But I think I miss you most of all at night. Every time I reach over to your side of the bed, you're not there. I feel so alone and empty without you next to me.

We are going to visit you when Brenda finishes work at 5:30. That will give you plenty of time to rest up before we get there! I'm not asking for you to do cartwheels, not yet at least. I just want to see you more alert. I know you can do it. I have faith in you baby. We'll get through this together. You just have to work with me. We are all here for you and we will never leave you. We love you baby... I love you!

Well, you opened your eyes for quite a long time tonight. Still not responsive though. The nurse said that, starting tomorrow, they will be reducing the anti seizure meds to 50%, three times per day. I really think that will help you wake up. Daniel made me all misty today. He told you, "Mom, you were always here for me, now I'm going to be here for you."

Rod 01/04/12

I was really hoping that you would be considerably more awake and alert today since they started taking your seizure meds down. I was extremely depressed when we saw you and there was even less eye opening, etc. The reality of everything is sinking in. I haven't talked to you in two weeks. I can't believe how much I miss you. My heart aches... I need you to wake up. I need to see some kind of hope that we will still have a life together. Please open your eyes and respond... you are hurting me. There are times when I just want to scream. This should not be happening... not to you!

Today is Amanda's birthday. We had a little get together with Mike and Dan, and Keith and his girlfriend at your mom and dad's house. We picked up a real nice cake for her. Wish you were here with us. I'm sure there were many other things going on today, but all I can think about is you.

Rod 01/05/12

I couldn't stand looking at my mustache anymore, so I finally shaved it off.

Just got a call from your nurse at the hospital. He said that the pulmonologist wanted to talk to me. I have the feeling that he will be talking about doing a trach on you because you've been on the respirator for so long. Jackie and I will be going to the hospital shortly.

I talked to the doctor. Not good news. He said that by dropping the meds to where they are, you should be much more alert and responsive. He believes that what we are seeing now, is due to brain damage. He said that your inability to move your arms and legs is also due to brain damage. I asked if the damage could be repaired, and he seemed to indicate that it is possible. He said he has seen people fully recover, partially recover, and not recover at all. Real encouraging words... it breaks my heart to see you laying in bed like this.

This has got to be a bad dream. It just can't be happening. I love you baby... We'll get thru this. The doctor said it could be weeks, if not months before we see any improvement. I'm hoping that you are able to get through this. That we are able to get through this... No matter how long it takes. The house, the car, the retirement, it all means nothing without you in my life. I need you to come back to me.

Today is Paul's birthday. I'm just not sure what to expect with my visit to you today. The doctor called early today and said that they wanted to do some kind of bronchial tube type of surgery because you have a lot of crud (that's my scientific term) in your lungs that they want to be able to drain. He said that they would be giving you small doses of propofol and some other stuff so I thoroughly expect you to be sleeping through my visit. The doctor also said they will be putting you on antibiotics because of some infection in your lungs. At least when they do the surgery you'll be able to take that damn tube out of your mouth and throat. He said that if the respirator is in your throat too long, it could mess with your vocal cords. I was trying to decide if that was a bad thing or not ha-ha. I would kill to hear your voice right now, even if you nagged at me.

When Breni and I got to your room for our visit, there were some nurses in there behind a closed curtain cleaning you up. We heard one of them ask "Are you smiling?" Well, I don't think I've ever seen Brenda move that fast in my life! She was in the room flinging the curtain open before I could even blink. When we got in your room you were wide awake, and you stayed awake for our whole visit. It looked like you're tracking us ever so slightly with your eyes. We think that you recognized us when we were talking to you. You smiled several times. We both agreed that you were smiling in response to things that we were saying to you like, "Rick and Brenda are bidding on a house right next door to us, so we'll be neighbors." We also told you that Mickaela (granddaughter) misses you so much, etc. You smiled several times. It just made our day. Hell it made our last two weeks! As depressed as I was yesterday, that's how happy you made me today... keep fighting baby!

Brenda email update 01/06/12

Last night's visit with Pam was hard. We couldn't get her to wake up. I took her hand and just sobbed. As soon as I started crying she opened her eyes. Only for a moment though. However, I was able to see her eyes.

The Journal

Brenda email update 01/09/12

I had a good visit with Pam, we actually saw her smile several times. She smiles at some of the things that we're saying, as well as when we asked her to. We were all on cloud nine! Since Friday we haven't been able to wake her up. Yesterday she was very swollen. I was shocked to see how large her arms, legs and middle area was. They did an ultrasound last night on her belly, and found that she has an enlarged liver. It's something that they're just going to watch. We're trying not to worry too much. This morning they're putting in a trachea, and removing the ventilator.

Brenda email update 01/11/12

Pam remains in ICU. She had an ultrasound, as well as an EEG, and they tested her for infection. The ultrasound was checking for blood clots, and that came back negative! She is being treated for a low blood pressure, and they seem to have that under control. The EEG test is not back yet. They have had her in sleep sedation for three days now. So, the visits are difficult; however, we continue to whisper in her ear that we are here, and love her very much. She just looks like she is sleeping.

Brenda email update 01/13/12

We met with the doctor yesterday and he confirmed that an incident happened on January 10th. He said that she had kidney and liver failure, as well as some brain damage.

They believe that she had a heart attack. At that meeting he didn't know what caused this incident. However; today, Sunday we were told it was thought that staph infection caused the incident. They have again taken her off of diuretic medication due to losing electrolytes. They were giving her potassium thru her feeding tube when we were there. She is so bloated; however, the doctor told us that it is just cosmetic and not to worry about that. It's hard not to worry when she's probably 40 pounds heavier than the day she went into the hospital.

I did request that a case manager call Rod. We were told that she will call tomorrow, which will be on Monday. I complained that we were not informed of this incident that happened on January 10th. Rod was told that she had a heart attack and is lucky to be alive; however, the heart doctor has not been in touch with Rod, or any of us. We have only been able to talk to the pulmonary doctor.

Brenda email update 01/19/12

During the first couple of visits with Pam, Rick and Rod noticed that she looked like she focused on Rod. Mom, Keith and I went to the 5:30 p.m. visit. When we walked into the room I said, "Hi Pam." She opened her eyes, then closed them for the remaining 30 minutes of our visits. I tickled her chin, and she smiled. She is still on anti seizure medication, which can cause her to sleep.

They're talking about putting Pam in a long term care facility. They say she may be moved as soon as Monday. That's good news. That tells me that she's stable enough to be moved out of ICU to a specialized hospital. She has been at Parkwest Hospital, in intensive care, for 27 days! I am excited to think that they are thinking she's ready to be moved out of ICU.

Pam's son's had to return to Arizona this past Tuesday. I am concerned that when Rick and I return to Omaha, that there will be gaps in visiting with Pam. Pam and I have a good friend from high school that lives in Knoxville. Linda Angel Simmons has offered to visit her when Rick and I return to Omaha. I am very thankful to Linda.

Brenda email update 01/23/12

Dad finally had an opportunity to visit Pam, he had been unable due to his oxygen. She recognized his voice. Dad told her that when she got out of the hospital he would have a BIG party for her. She smiled from ear to ear. Mom said she smiled so big you could see her teeth.

On the second visit, mom told Pam it was time to go, and Pam looked as if she was going to cry. Mom told her not to cry, but to give her a kiss, so Pam puckered her lips. She can definitely hear us.

Linda Angel Simmons (high school friend) 01/25/12 email to Brenda

Pam seemed to be more comfortable tonight than she has been. She looks very rested. She smiled a lot. After I sang to her, I made the comment that I wasn't a very good singer, and she really smiled big. I think she was agreeing with me. I laughed!

Linda Angel Simmons 02/01/12 email to Brenda

Just wanted to let you know that Pam has been sleeping the last two nights. The nurse had just given her pain meds, so she was knocked out. She looks great and the swelling is continuing to go down, so that's good. Any news on your end? The nurse did say that she thought the family was looking into taking her back to Arizona. She said it would probably take awhile for everything to get approved.

I think about you every single day and pray that you'll be strong and patient through all of this. I know how close you and Pam have always been and I can't imagine what you must be feeling. I am so looking forward to seeing you next week. I hope you know that we would love for you to stay with us if you need. We have more than enough room and you could work from here and be so close to the hospital.

Linda Angel Simmons 02/03/12 email to Brenda

Brenda,

You are so precious to me! You don't know how much you and Pam have blessed my life too. I still can't help but to believe that Pam is healing and will be able to communicate with everyone in time. The nurse was telling me about people who have been declared brain dead and have come back. She also said that she asked Pam to blink twice if she wanted pain meds and she blinked twice. I think that is amazing!!! We just need to continue to hope for the best and pray for whatever God has in his plan for Pam. Only he knows what will happen. Patience, patience, patience, at this point is what we need. My heart goes out to your parents, it must be so hard for them too. Sorry for babbling. A little too much coffee this morning. I can't wait to see you. Love and hugs! Linda

Brenda email update 02/05/12

I made it to Tennessee! I left on Saturday about 4:30 a.m.. Arrived at my parents home about 8 p.m.. I was on a mission to get there without spending the night. I was afraid if I spent the night I may not get to see Pam on Sunday due to her dialysis schedule. We have to call the hospital every morning to find out what time they planned to do dialysis, which can interrupt our visitation.

February 05, 2012 makes 43 days that Pam has been at Parkwest Hospital in the ICU. It seems like an eternity, yet I can't believe that she is there. Some of our family went to the visitation on Sunday. It was the best day yet! During the first visit, she was sleeping a lot; however, the next visit was awesome. Rod asked her to smile for me and she gave me the biggest smile! He also asked her to wiggle her toes and she did twice. We keep trying to get her to squeeze our hands, or give us any kind of movement, which is not happening yet. Pam looked like she was trying to tell us something. Her face was very expressive, and she was moving her lips. We were thrilled to see this.

Our friend, Linda Angel Simmons, has visited Pam every day, and sometimes twice a day since I was gone. Linda is such a blessing to our family's lives! We can't thank her enough for all that she has done! Linda came to the hospital today to see me. We plan to meet immediately after visitation. I asked the nurses if Linda and I could sneak back in for a moment and they gave us permission. Linda said, "Pam, I'm going to sing to you today" Pam smiled real big, as if she wanted to laugh. Linda asked her if she wanted her face wiped with a cool cloth and again Pam gave a great big smile. Linda has been putting chap stick on Pam's lips. She asked Pam if she wanted some chap stick and Pam made a face as if to say, "No way!" We had a good laugh.

Even though Linda told her she wasn't going to sing, we sang to Pam. She had a big smile on her face. I can't tell you how much I enjoyed this visit with her! I am so looking forward to our next visit.

Brenda email update 02/07/12

Another good visit with Pam! Rod received a call from the nurse saying that Pam did not do well when they drained the two liters of fluid from her lungs. They needed his permission to put her on 24 hour dialysis for four days.

When we arrived at the hospital, she was wide awake. For the first time, they had her lying on her side. When Pam is awake, she is mostly looking straight ahead; however, she did look right at me for a moment last night! Linda walked toward her and Rod noticed that she was focusing on Linda. She moved her mouth a few times as if she were trying to tell us something; however, not nearly as much as the day before.

The big moment came when the nurse told Rod that she heard Pam say, "I can't breathe." That happened just before we got there. The nurse gave Pam a shot to make her more comfortable, so she was very tired by the end of our visit.

Just before leaving the room, Linda put some flavored chap stick on Pam, and you could tell that she really liked it because she licked her lips.

Brenda email update 02/11/12

I'm so excited to give you this update on Pam! She has made tremendous progress this week. She's moving her arms and legs and really trying to talk through her breathing tube. We can only understand a couple of words; water, and that she wants to go home. We asked her what she thought Tiffany was having and she mouthed, "girl," two different times. She is awake during most of our visits, and she is very focused on whoever is speaking to her. She was a little frustrated during a couple of our visits because she kept trying to tell us something and we couldn't understand what she was saying. When our short 30 minute visit is over, she turns her head to watch us leave. That is very hard for me.

Two days ago, she talked the entire 30 minutes. When we walked out, we were talking to the nurse and I heard her yell what I thought was "Bren!" She yelled really loud; Rod and I were very surprised.

Our dear friend Linda Angel Simmons, continues to visit with Pam. Linda knows just what to do to make her comfortable. When Linda walks into the room Pam lights up! She smiles and lifts her eyebrows. It's awesome to see her react to Linda like that!

I told Pam that her granddaughter, "Mickaela" asks about her and that she loves her very much. She will smile from ear to ear whenever she hears about Mickaela and her other grandchildren. I've given her messages from Rick, Aunt Linda, Claudia, Julie and everyone else who sends her messages. She always smiles when hearing about friends and family. I have asked her to give me a kiss and she puckers up. It's obvious she knows what we're saying!

Brenda email update 02/16/12

Mom and dad went to visit Pam today. They had her in a chair before mom and dad got there for about two hours! That was awesome! She was in pain, so they gave her

The Journal

something to ease the pain, so she slept through the second visit. They were just happy to see her.

I called and talked to her caseworker Tuesday. They're going to try to get her into the Select Rehab in Phoenix. The doctor just told Kay, the case worker, yesterday that she is doing really well and that she is more than ready for rehab!

Pam is going back to Arizona soon! They approved her to go to a rehab called Select One, which is one of the best rehabs in Arizona. We are just waiting for them to pull the trigger with a medical jet to transport she and Rod.

My visits are getting better and better. We can understand some of the words that she is speaking. Last night she told Rod and I, "They throw me around like a rag doll." That brought me to tears because she looked like she was going to cry. She told our friend Linda, "Watch out for that nurse!" The nurse had just given her a shot.

Our prayers are finally being answered. She is doing so much better than any of the doctors and nurses expected. They gave her a gift bag today. The gift bag had a Parkwest t-shirt, a Tennessee hat and a stuffed animal. The staff was awesome, even though she told Linda to watch out for that nurse! Lol Thank you for your continued prayers.

Mom 02/23/12

Hi honey, I have not done any writing to date because I just wanted to step back and think about what all I wanted to say.

This has just been a ride that has been unbelievable. We have so many people to thank. People we do not know and people we have not met. They all want to pray for you and have added you to their prayer chains. Your family and friends are praying for you as well. You are so loved and admired. God has really watched over you and you have worked so hard to get well.

You will most likely leave Tennessee today to go to Arizona. Dad and I will miss you so much, but we know that you going home is super important, so it's okay with us. God will keep you safe. We love you with all of our hearts. Mom & Dad

Brenda email update 03/05/12

After 70 days ICU at Parkwest Hospital, Pam was able to fly back to Arizona on Saturday. They flew her to St Joseph Hospital in Phoenix. The flight took both Rod and Pam, and she said it was the worst flight she had ever been on. It took about six hours, and she was in a lot of pain. She is doing so much better with each passing day. I actually talked to her on the phone for about 30 seconds. It was awesome. It didn't sound like her, however she still has her sense of humor. The first thing she said to me was, "Good morning sunshine." That was something that I have missed hearing her say to me every morning! She told me she was so happy to be back in Arizona. She also told me it was the flight from hell.

The Journal

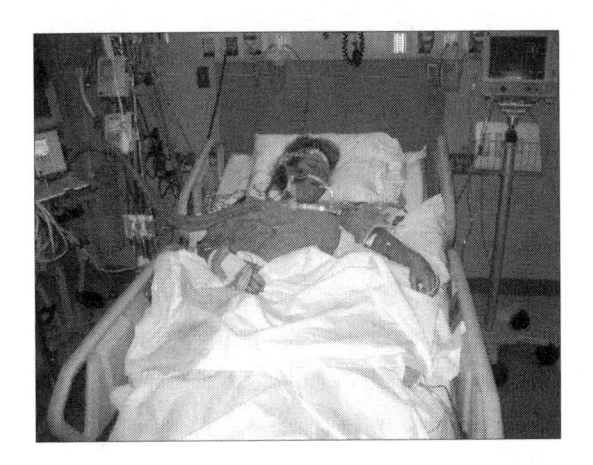

Earlier in the week she had her first meal. She also was allowed to have a Diet Coke. Rod said that he is sure that Coke stocks have tumbled since Pam wasn't able to have it for over two months!

Many thanks to Linda Angel Simmons for visiting Pam every day and evening. Also thank you to Rose and Lance for visiting Pam from Ohio. Thank you all for your thoughts and prayers! She's on her way to recovery which is a miracle. The majority of people who have had aortic dissections did not survive. I have you to thank for keeping her in your prayers. Life is good!

I am so lucky to have a sister like Pam. Last year she gave me a little laminated card that I keep in my purse.

More Than Sisters

What are the chances that of all the zillion people in the world God would see fit to make us sisters? The common bond between us goes far beyond mere bloodlines. We find joy in each other's triumph's, and sorrow in each other's pain. We are so much more than sisters, we are also friends.

This concludes the journal and email entries.

CHAPTER 14

Waking Up

I really can't remember when I finally woke up.

I remember bits and pieces, but nothing distinctive.

I don't know if I ever really asked what had happened to me, or how long I had been in the hospital. I came to understand things very slowly in the beginning, with the help of my family.

For the longest time, I had no idea how close I had come to dying. It took weeks before I came to the realization that I had been and in some ways was still knocking on death's door.

When I heard the percentage of those who survive an aortic dissection, I was shocked. By God's grace I fell into the, "Less than 5% survival rate range."

When I first awoke and since I had had a tracheotomy, I had a difficult time talking and communicating with everyone. I was very frustrated when they couldn't understand me, however, this was just a small problem compared to the numerous issues I was facing. I couldn't walk. I couldn't use my hands. I couldn't feed myself. I was literally bed ridden. I knew I would have months, if not years, of therapy ahead of me.

I remember being very confused about what was real and what was not because of the dreams that I was having while I was in the coma. I could not distinguish between reality and dreams.

I had been awake for two weeks and the entire time I thought that my granddaughter, Mickaela, had been murdered. It was something that I didn't want to discuss with my family because I didn't want to have to think about it.

Finally, one day, Rod mentioned Mickaela's name and I said, "She's gone."

Rod said, "What do you mean she's gone, she's in Alaska."

I said, "No she isn't, she was murdered!"

Again, Rod insisted that she was alive and well. I just broke down and cried. They were tears of happiness. It was all just a nightmare, a horrible, horrible nightmare.

Waking Up

I remembered seeing Rod dressed like a doctor. He would come into my room and talk to the nurses as if he knew exactly what was going on. I felt very embarrassed by his actions and didn't want the nurses to know that he was my husband. He would speak with a southern accent, just like the nurses from Tennessee did. It wasn't until later that I realized it was all a dream.

I was sure that the medication I was on had something to do with the fact that my dreams seemed so real.

I so looked forward to going home to Arizona. Before I left Parkwest Hospital, the infectious disease doctor came into my room to make me aware that my arm had become infected with MRSA (Methicillin - Restraint Staphylococcus Aureus). This was directly related to a bad pick line.

The doctor said that they wouldn't be treating the MRSA at Parkwest, but rather at the hospital I would be going to in Arizona. Originally, the doctors thought I would be leaving the hospital in a few days, however, I remained there for two more weeks. As a result, when I arrived in Arizona I had to have three surgeries on my left arm in order to save it.

The doctor in Arizona told me if it had been any longer, they would have had to amputate my arm. The infection had spread so much that they removed two golf ball size chunks of infection from my arm.

The doctors would only allow me to fly home from Tennessee to Arizona on a medical jet. Rod spent nearly two weeks arguing with the insurance company to cover the $19,000 it cost to fly me home.

The insurance company never did agree to pay, so we had to pay for the jet out of our own pocket.

On March 3rd, I flew back to Arizona.

The jet carried the pilot, co-pilot, two medical personnel, Rod and I. I was laying on a bed that had a one-inch thick cover. It was like laying on a hard board.

The flight lasted six agonizing hours, before we finally landed at Phoenix Sky Harbor Airport. Once there, I was put into an ambulance and taken to St Joseph's Hospital in Phoenix.

St Joseph's Hospital is well known for their "State of the Art" rehab facility. People from around the world come to St Joseph's Hospital, based on their reputation for rehabilitation.

When we arrived at the hospital I was taken directly to my new room. It was the room I would remain in for the next two and a half months.

CHAPTER 15

The Long Road To Recovery

I arrived on a Saturday afternoon, so I had the rest of that day and Sunday to prepare for a grueling day of therapy on Monday. I was scheduled for physical therapy (PT), speech therapy (ST), and occupational therapy (OT), which I would do Monday through Friday. I would spend three hours each day in therapy, working toward my recovery.

It was such a very slow process. It took what seemed like a tremendous amount of time for me to see any gains.

I thought that Speech Therapy (ST) would be easy, but it turned out to be surprisingly difficult. I had to learn how to breathe all over again. I couldn't say more than two words without running out of breath.

For me, that was tough. I had always loved to talk, it would be a long time before I could carry on a normal conversation.

It was even harder for me to talk on the phone, so I didn't really want to talk to anybody. I know that this was difficult for my family to understand. They were used to talking to me on the phone every single day. Now I was avoiding their calls.

When I got out of bed to go to the therapy room, I had to be hoisted out of bed with a crane-like machine which had a canvas seat attached to it. From there I was placed in a wheelchair and headed to the therapy room. This was a very large room where many other patients would also have their therapy.

There I would have my PT (Physical Therapy) and OT, (Occupational Therapy).

In PT the therapist would begin by working my leg muscles. Since I hadn't walked in over two and a half months I had no muscle strength in my legs. I wouldn't have been able to walk even if I had wanted to.

OT seemed especially difficult for me, my fingers were all curled under. I assumed it was caused by the strokes, but I never found out. It was intensely painful when they worked on my fingers. My left hand seemed to be worse than my right hand, which was fortunate for me as a righty.

The Long Road To Recovery

The days seemed to go slow while I was at St Joseph's Hospital. Rod visited me every single day, for at least a couple of hours. On the weekends some of my friends would come by and visit me as well. I couldn't wait to go home. There's nothing like home.

Toward the end of my stint at St Joseph's Hospital, I began to learn how to walk again.

In the beginning, I took maybe 5 steps with a walker. I remember asking a male therapist if I would ever be able to walk again by myself in the beginning of my therapy and he said, "That's up to you." I remember thinking about his answer and I thought, he is right, it was up to me.

So from that day on I knew I would walk again. In fact, I was walking down to the nurses' station and back by the time I left the hospital.

Before I could leave Saint Joseph's Hospital I had to go through a procedure to drain my lungs. I was informed that I had one liter of fluid on each lung. They gave me a choice of having one lung drained one day and the other the following day. I decided to have them done at the same time. I asked the doctor if there were any risks involved, and he said "Yes" he could possibly puncture my lungs, but that was very rare.

The doctor had me sit on a table while he started the procedure using a needle approximately 12 inches long. The procedure was very painful, as he had to insert the needle into my back. It hurt so bad that I decided to have the other lung done the following day. After he finished, I was taken to an observation room where they monitored my vitals.

Soon after being taken to the room, I began to have difficulty breathing. It scared me so bad that I began to hyperventilate. The nurses ran into my room and realized there was a problem, so they brought the doctor back to my room. He quickly sent me for an X-ray, and soon discovered he had punctured my lung. All the while I was gasping for air.

I truly thought I was going to die that day. My mind raced, how could this happen? I had made it through the worst of things, and now this. I wasn't going to make it through this one.

I felt so alone. I wished Rod was there with me, but he was in the waiting area and wasn't allowed to come back and see me.

I found myself praying like never before.

After realizing what he had done, the doctor had to perform another procedure. This time he had to insert a tube into my chest.

The next day I had to have the other lung drained. I was so afraid that the same thing would happen again. I hoped that this time would be different.

The Long Road To Recovery

When I entered the room for the second procedure I saw a different doctor which filled me with relief. As it turned out the second procedure was a complete success.

I was honored to receive a wonderful letter from my nephew about my journey. I have to admit that it lifted my spirits and I wanted to include in here:

"Uncle Rod and Aunt Pam,

"It was so great to see you guys last weekend! Aunt Pam you are so inspirational, I couldn't be more blessed to witness you working so hard to try and get back to 100%! I have never seen someone who has had to face so much adversity in such a short period of time, yet, through hard work and determination you are more than succeeding. I am so proud of you; on Friday when I watched you go through all of your physical and speech therapy I wanted to cry tears of joy the entire time. When I first got there you were already walking and you took at least 75 steps that day, Sheeba said you were just showing off for me because you hadn't walked that far yet and I am so grateful I got to see every step! I thought that may have been it but then you went even further and rode the bike for 8 minutes which was 2 minutes longer than you were supposed to. Time and time again you exceed expectations, keep that up Aunt Pam all this hard work will make you get better even faster. Next, you had speech therapy, which was just as impressive as you

The Spirit Within Me

walking, pretty sure Uncle Rod and I didn't even know the answer to a few of the jumbled word sentences. The best part of your speech therapy was watching you try to pull a fast one past your teacher. Then looking at her like an innocent little kid to see if she was paying attention to the words that you purposely left out! Uncle Rod and I were laughing so hard! The most memorable moment of the day though, was to hear you call Uncle Rod an ass! I couldn't have been happier to hear those words come out of your mouth again; it was like music to my ears!

"What I witnessed in Arizona was nothing short of a miracle considering the last time I saw you was in Tennessee and you were hooked up to what seemed to be 50 machines! I will never forget that day, I was holding your hand as you laid on the bed and I told you how much I love you and how everything would be okay. I have had no doubt in my mind since Christmas Eve at 10:30 a.m. when this horrific event happened that you would overcome as you always do. You're a fighter Aunt Pam and you were meant to beat this. You have hundreds of people that are praying for you and the full recovery that you will make.

"Uncle Rod, thank you so much for being the loving, caring, and supportive husband that you are to my Aunt. She is very blessed to have someone like you in her life. You have been by her side day after day doing everything you can to see that she gets back to 100%. I cannot begin to imagine how tough it must be to see your wife, the person you love most in your life in the hospital for the last 5 months. It takes a great deal of courage to continue to stay so positive like you have in this tough time. I am grateful to have seen through you two how a marriage should be, and what love is all about.

"I want to thank-you guys again for everything you have done for me! You two have truly been a second set of parents for me and I will always be grateful for that. I wish I could be there in Arizona helping out day in and day out. Since I unfortunately cannot do that I thought and prayed for a long time on how I could help. I want to give you guys some money. I worked hard for 72 straight days to earn this money. Please accept this, it would really and truly hurt my feelings if you didn't because I did this for you guys and wouldn't have been able to if you weren't the motivation behind it. One of my clients donated $100 as well. I cannot wait to see you guys again in August I love you both so much!"

CHAPTER 16

Going Home

I really developed a good relationship with all of the nurses and therapists at St Joseph's Hospital. I have them to thank for giving me a big boost on my road to recovery. Their encouragement gave me the strength to work very hard, never giving up and never giving in.

After 69 days in the hospital at St Joseph's, I went home.

It was so wonderful to be at home again with Rod and my puppies, Ernest T and Charlene. I had missed my home. I learned how much home is truly a place where I felt safe and comfortable. It was the home that Rod and I bought together and decorated together. It was beautiful. It was a place that I felt at peace. I was where I should be. I was finally home.

My mom and dad decided to come out to Arizona to help out once I came home. My mom combed my hair and would put it in a ponytail. She also shaved my legs. Those were the things that I needed most from my mom. Sure Rod could do those things for me, but my mom had that special touch.

My dad would cook for me. He always loved to cook. At 80 years old that was the one thing that he was able to do for me. It was so special. He took pride in everything he cooked, whether it was a fancy dish, or something simple.

My dad had been a cook in the army while he served in Korea. His love for cooking carried over when he left the military. It was so wonderful to have my parents there in Arizona with me. Just having them there was awesome. It just reaffirmed how much they loved me.

At that time there were so many things that I was dependent upon someone else doing for me.

I was still learning how to walk again. I felt so determined not to use a walker or a cane, as I was afraid that I would get used to it and it would become, literally, a crutch. I wanted to walk alone, by myself, without any assistance. That was very important to me.

I had to learn how to get up and down from a chair or couch. It literally took weeks before I was able to do it on my own. Weeks upon weeks of practicing and building my muscle strength in order to get up from a chair was unbelievable to me.

I soon realized how much I had taken for granted. Everything I did now would be a struggle. My life would never again be the same.

I had to eat with a strap around my hand, which would hold my utensils. My fingers were still in a "claw" like position, which made it impossible to hold a fork or spoon. Just to sit down and eat a meal was a chore.

I felt handicapped for the first time in my life.

I needed assistance with just about everything that I did. It was a feeling that I did not like, not one bit.

Our house is a two story. We put a hospital bed in our den downstairs. That is where I slept.

This was rough because I couldn't sleep with Rod now and I missed the closeness we once had. The tender moments we shared would have to be temporarily postponed until much later. Rod was always such a loving husband and I knew he understood and would be patient with me.

Unfortunately there was only a half bath on the first floor, without a shower or tub.

So the challenge before me was to learn how to climb the stairs. Rod would stand directly behind me on the way up the stairs and in front of me on the way down. It was time-consuming, like everything was now. If I wanted a shower I had to climb the stairs.

My shoulder had been very painful since I came out of the coma in the hospital in Tennessee. Several months after I came home from St Joseph's, I had an x-ray done and discovered that my left shoulder was dislocated.

I remember telling Breni and Rod, "They throw me around like a rag doll," when I was at Parkwest Hospital. It's very possible that when the nurses were moving me around, they were rougher than they realized.

Because of this I now had one more obstacle in my way because I couldn't lift my left arm at all. My shoulder would require surgery to repair the damage that had been done.

I waited a year and a half before having surgery. It wasn't that I was just putting it off, I had so many other things that took priority. Since it was my left shoulder, I wasn't as concerned about having it being repaired as I was concentrating on my right side.

My right shoulder and hand took first priority. If I could get that side working again, I'd be in business.

My OT therapist, Scot McCoy, worked with me diligently in order for me to live a functional life. He had come highly recommended and he certainly lived up to and beyond my expectations.

CHAPTER 17

The Setback

I had been home from the hospital for two months when I decided to climb the stairs alone.

I told Rod that I wanted to take a nap upstairs in my own bed, so he headed upstairs to get the bed ready. While I was waiting downstairs, I made the decision to climb the stairs by myself and surprise Rod.

How hard could it be? I had done it a million times before my aortic dissection. I wanted to prove to myself, as well as Rod, that I was getting better.

The first two steps went as planned, but when I got to the third step I lost my grip on the railing.

Without the full use of my hand I didn't have a chance. I fell completely backwards and landed on the tile below on my back. The pain was excruciating. The pain was worse than anything that I have ever felt before. It was even more painful than when I broke my leg on the ledges. I screamed and Rod came running.

The look on his face scared me, he looked horrified. It was as if he was reliving my aortic dissection and all of those feelings rushed to the surface. He asked me what happened and I told him that I wanted to surprise him and climb the stairs by myself. He helped me up from the floor and into a chair.

I was crying from all of the pain. I couldn't believe how much I was hurting. Rod scolded me and told me I shouldn't have tried to climb the stairs alone. Even though I understood how scared he was, the last thing I needed at that time was a lecture. It was only four o'clock in the afternoon, all I wanted to do was go to bed.

However, I was in so much pain I couldn't sleep. My back was hurting like never before. I felt that I had to make it until the morning before going to the hospital because the last thing that I wanted to do was to wake Rod in the middle of the night to take me. I know that he would have gladly taken me to the emergency room (ER), but I felt so guilty.

At six o'clock in the morning I couldn't take the pain any longer and decided to go to the hospital. Rod helped me out of bed, got me dressed and we headed to the ER.

The Setback

After we checked in, we were taken back to a private room where I would be seen by a doctor. The doctor asked me a series of questions and then he ordered a CAT scan. The results of the scan were devastating. I had a T1, T2 and T3 compression fracture and this meant that I had broken my back.

I felt sick, I couldn't believe what I had just done to myself. What would have been a simple climb up the stairs in my prior life turned out to be devastating. This would, no doubt, set me back in my recovery.

I was taken to a rehab hospital where I would remain for the next three weeks. I can't remember much of the first several days because I was heavily medicated for the pain. I couldn't believe I was back in the hospital again so soon after being released from St Joseph's Hospital.

I was fitted into a back brace that I was required to wear for the next six weeks. Week two of my stay at the hospital I began therapy. Therapy basically consisted of getting out of bed and walking for 30 minutes each day. The rest of the day I was stuck in bed with nothing to do but watch television.

The days dragged on very slowly.

Rod came to visit me every day for a couple of hours, which helped pass the time. I was counting down the days until I could go home. After three weeks, I was finally released to go home, it couldn't have come soon enough.

One month after returning home we invited my friend Lynn over for a visit. Lynn had been a dear friend of mine for over 20 years. We were sitting on our patio reminiscing about things that we had been through over the years. I had to go to the bathroom so I excused myself and headed to the bathroom. Rod got up and followed me, in order to help me with my pants. He left the bathroom and closed the door. I was sitting on my riser seat when I inadvertently leaned to the right. In an instant, the seat came off and dumped me onto the floor. I hit my head on the sink on the way down and landed in front of the door.

I screamed and Rod came running. He tried to open the door, but was unable because my body was blocking the door. I tried to move out of the way, but was unable. I cracked my head open on the sink and it was bleeding heavily. All Rod could see was blood flowing under the door and he couldn't get to me.

He told Lynn to call 911. Then he ran outside and around to the side yard and broke the bathroom window. Rod was able to climb in through the window and move me away from the door. He pulled me out of the bathroom and into the kitchen while we waited for the paramedics.

The paramedics arrived within minutes. They loaded me into a waiting ambulance and headed to the hospital. Once

The Setback

there, they assessed the damage and proceeded to put 10 stitches in my head.

Unlike the two previous trips to the hospital, I didn't have to stay overnight this time.

CHAPTER 18

Finding Strength

I admit after all these trials, I found myself feeling very depressed just knowing the struggles I had ahead of me.

I wondered why God spared my life, knowing I would be so challenged. How would I overcome the obstacles before me? My hands were basically useless. My left shoulder was dislocated and useless as well. I could walk, but I felt dizzy, as if my equilibrium was off. Falling was a risk that I took every time I got up and walked. I could no longer drive. I was even unable to put my own seatbelt on.

I felt trapped inside my own body because of all of the things I could no longer do. I was frustrated at every turn. I couldn't even dress myself, or clean myself after using the bathroom. I had to remove any feelings of embarrassment by having Rod help me with these things. It was a life very different from the one I had once known. My independence was gone. Facing life now just seemed dreadful.

As vain as it might sound, not being able to do my makeup or hair pained my pride. Those who know me know that I take pride in the way that I look. I wouldn't go to the mailbox without putting my makeup on before I had my aortic dissection. This was something that really bothered me.

I had to rely on Rod to do my hair. There would be no blow drying or using the curling iron. He just didn't know how to do those things and I couldn't expect him to know. The days of me being meticulous about the way I looked were gone. I no longer could be the vain person that I had been. It was very humbling.

I had to remind myself that I was alive, and where there's life, there is hope.

Maybe God wanted me to find myself and love me for who I am, stripped of makeup and pretty hair. I had to see myself raw and unassuming.

For the first time I had to see who I truly was inside. I had to find the strength to overcome the devastating reality of what had happened to me.

This would, no doubt, be my test of inner strength and will to get better. I would have to take my therapy seriously and work my butt off if I wanted to get better. I knew if I ever wanted to do my own makeup and hair, I really had to work hard, harder than I ever could have imagined. That was my job now since I was retired.

I had a year and a half before Rod would retire and we could start enjoying life, if I was ready.

We had so many plans for our retirement prior to my getting sick. We wanted to travel without time restrictions so we could go anywhere and stay as long as we wanted. We planned to buy a cabin by a lake and enjoy the summers there, rather than spending the summers in Phoenix where the temperature can be as high as 121°. We wanted someplace where we could sit on the front porch in the evening and go boating during the day. A place where we could enjoy everything we had worked so hard for.

Part of my lessons included knowing that no matter how bad my life was now, I could always look around and see someone else worse off. Every trip I made to my rehab doctor I would see a paraplegic, or a child confined to a wheelchair. Most of these children don't even realize their dilemma. They can't walk, talk, or even think. It's at that very moment that I realized how blessed I was, and I was forced to stop feeling sorry for myself.

With these trials I had learned humility and love for myself at the same time. Such a combination only being a gift from God.

CHAPTER 19

July 4th

Brenda and Rick decided to host a Fourth of July party at their home in Nebraska and invited friends and relatives from all over the country. We made plans to go and spend the holiday with my family. This would be the first time ever that we would be spending time with my sister over the 4th of July. My mom and dad planned to go as well. Rod's daughter Jennifer had just had a baby boy so we were going to go to South Carolina from Nebraska to see our new grand baby.

It would be my first trip since I had the aortic dissection. I was really looking forward to it.

My mom and dad decided to leave on Saturday for Nebraska. They took a shuttle to the airport and when they

The Spirit Within Me

were only two miles away, my dad got very ill. The shuttle driver pulled off to the side of the road. My dad's lips were blue from a lack of oxygen.

He had been on an oxygen machine because he had mesothelioma. He worked around asbestos for 30 years at his job not knowing the dangers involved. The airline had a rule that oxygen machines cannot be set at a level higher than a 4. My dad required a 6, so he wasn't receiving the amount of oxygen that he needed the entire trip. The shuttle driver called 911 and they waited for an ambulance.

My dad was taken to the local hospital where he stayed overnight. The following day he was transported to a hospital closer to his home. When I talked to my dad he kept apologizing for missing our reunion in Nebraska. He said he really tried to make it.

I told him not to worry, that we would see him in Tennessee for Christmas. My dad was now in CCU (critical care unit) and we didn't know how long he would be there.

We went ahead and flew to Nebraska on Wednesday. It was so good to see my sister again. We were very concerned about my dad, but we did our best to enjoy our time together. The fireworks in Omaha were incredible. They are like nothing I have ever seen before. They start setting off fireworks on July 1st and continue until July 5th, going from early in the evening until late at night.

July 4th

My sister's house sits on a golf course and the windows in their living room span from one end of the wall to the other. It provided a great view for watching fireworks. We watched fireworks for hours, with a panoramic view. It was absolutely incredible.

On Saturday we received a call from my mom saying that the doctors didn't expect my dad to survive, and if he did, he would be sent to a nursing home. We knew we needed to fly to Tennessee. Brenda, Rod and I booked tickets for early Sunday morning. We had to cancel our trip to South Carolina to see our new grand baby, but our daughter understood that we needed to see our dad, for what might be the last time.

When we landed at the Nashville airport we jumped in our rental car and headed straight to the hospital. We felt an urgency to get there as quickly as possible. We didn't know if we would ever see him alive again.

Mom met us at the front door of the hospital. We asked her how he was doing and she said he was holding his own.

When we got to his room he looked as if he were sleeping. They had him heavily sedated so that he would stay calm. I held his hand and told him I was here and how much I loved him. While he was unable to respond, I just wanted for him to know that I was there.

After a couple of hours we decided to go back to mom and dad's house. Brenda stayed the night at the hospital. My dad never liked being alone, so it was decided that someone would always stay the night with him. Hospital rules were that only one person could stay the night, so that meant that I couldn't stay. I wouldn't be able to get up and down from the chair because it sat so low, nor could I go to the bathroom without assistance. I wanted to be there for my dad but I was unable, which hurt me deep inside.

On Monday we got up and drove for an hour back to the hospital. We sat quietly with my dad for about an hour. A nurse came in and said that she was going to reduce his sedation medication. By doing so, he would most likely wake up and know that we were there.

After a short time, though unable to speak as he was on a ventilator, my dad started to open his eyes.

Brenda stood on one side of the bed and I was on the other side. We were both holding his hands when Brenda said, "Hi dad, I'm here." He had a look on his face that let us know he understood.

I said, "Dad, it's Pam, I'm here too."

Dad turned his head toward me and started to cry. Seeing our Dad crying brought Brenda and me to tears as well. My heart was breaking because I knew that my father wasn't long for this world.

July 4th

The nurse came running into the room and told us to back away from the bed because he was getting too excited. His numbers were going in a negative direction. Brenda and I moved about three feet away from his bed as we continued to sob. That brought the nurse back into the room and she sternly said, "Move over to the other side of the room." We reluctantly left his side.

Our dad had just given us the greatest gift he could have given.

He let us know that he knew we were there. That was so important. We wanted him to know how loved he was. My dad was an icon in my eyes and I believe that everyone else in the family felt the same way. He was so loving, generous and thoughtful. He could never be replaced.

Later that afternoon my mom, Brenda and Keith left the hospital to meet the overseer of the cemetery that my parents chose to be buried in. They went there to pick out the plots where they would be buried.

While they were gone the nurse decided to reduce dad's medication once again. I carefully got up from my chair and walked over to my dad's bed. I held his hand and told him how much I loved him and asked him to squeeze my hand if he understood. He immediately squeezed my hand. I was elated!

Rod got up and walked over to dad's bed and told my dad that he would always take care of me and not to worry about me. I do believe my dad understood him. When everyone returned from the cemetery, I shared the good news. My mom decided to stay the night with my dad so the rest of us returned home.

The next morning my mom returned home from the hospital. She wanted to get a couple of hours of sleep before going back. Brenda, Rod and I got ready to head to the hospital when the phone rang. It was the hospital. They said that we needed to head to the hospital as soon as possible, as my dad's vitals were very bad.

In a panic, we jumped in the car and raced to the hospital which was almost an hour away. We were about 20 minutes into our drive when my mom got the "dreaded" call. My dad had passed.

My dad, who had been my cheerleader my whole life, especially during the past year and a half, was now gone. The man who lived a long and happy life and whose generosity was like no other, was gone. Dad had such a great sense of humor. He made us laugh all the time. There was no doubt that he would be greatly missed.

When we arrived at the hospital we went straight to his room. The nurse said we could spend as much time with him as we needed.

July 4th

We walked into the room and the first thing I noticed was that he had been covered with his bright orange Tennessee Volunteer's blanket. I knew how much he loved his Volunteer's and was both happy and sad that this had been done for him. I walked over to my dad, kissed his head and told him I loved him and that I would miss him. The rest of the family said their goodbyes in a similar fashion. We spent about an hour with him before leaving for the mortuary. We now had a funeral to plan.

The ride home was somber. We all agreed that dad gave us the greatest gift he could've given us. He recognized us the day before he passed.

We also felt blessed that he didn't suffer much.

My mom said that when she stayed with him the night before, she told him it was okay to go to sleep. My dad knew it was okay to go. He knew we would all be okay. He was finally at peace.

My mom decided not to have a viewing but rather a graveside service. Because my dad was in the Armed Forces, we had a full military service. My dad would have been proud.

My dad had a long conversation with Jon, his grandson, a couple of weeks before he passed. I asked Jon how it came to be that his grandpa asked him to officiate his service.

He said, "I think grandpa gave me the honor of officiating his service because he knew how much he meant to me. He knew what a role model and father figure he was to me. He understood that he had an enormous impact on my life. He played such an integral role in raising me to be the man I am today.

"Grandpa knew I am a man of faith,. We talked for two hours a few weeks before he passed. The entire conversation was about God and what faith meant to both of us. It was a life- changing conversation that I will never forget. I believe after the conversation he felt it was the right time to ask me to officiate his service.

"It was important to him to have someone who he was close with and truly knew him to celebrate his life in front of the people he loved so much. It was the most important thing I have ever been asked to do. I felt so honored and humbled to do that for him. It was the most rewarding and toughest thing I have ever had to do."

Jon's service was perfect. He had us laughing and crying with some of the stories he told; it couldn't have been a nicer service. My mom said he was happier than he had ever been and for that she was grateful. She felt comforted by knowing that my dad was in heaven and had been prepared for it.

CHAPTER 20

Visiting

While I was in Tennessee, I decided to go visit Dr. Maggart (my heart surgeon) and the staff at Parkwest Hospital.

Our first stop was Dr. Maggart's office. I began to shake when I saw him. Here was the man who was responsible for saving my life. We both teared up as we hugged each other. I thanked him for everything he had done to spare my life. He just smiled from ear to ear. I don't know how often he has patients come back to visit, but I owed him that. He was my hero. I honestly think that he did not expect me to survive and that he was a little surprised that I did. We chatted for about 10 minutes, then we left for the hospital.

Dr. Maggart called ahead and told the staff in CCU that we were on our way. When we got there, they were

The Spirit Within Me

all waiting. It was simply amazing, seeing the eight to ten nurses that took care of me. Once again, there were lots of tears. This time they were tears of joy. I recognized some of them, but not all of them.

One nurse that I did recognize was nurse Melody. She gave me a pedicure the day before I left the hospital. That will always stay with me, just knowing how much they cared about me. I will forever be grateful to Dr. Maggart and the CCU staff at Parkwest Hospital.

Dr. Maggart will always have a special place in my heart. Christmas 2012, I sent him a Christmas card. I wanted to tell him how much I appreciated everything that he did for me. He literally saved my life. I included a picture of myself standing in front of my Christmas tree. I wanted him to see how far I had come since he last saw me. I received a hand written letter back from him.

"Dear Mrs. Meintel,"

"I was absolutely thrilled to get a Christmas card from you and was delighted to see how beautiful you looked in front of your Christmas tree. The ICU people were also very pleased to hear from you. We are grateful to your husband for helping with the writing".

"I hope you are aware that you were one of our favorite patients ever and we often think about you and talk of you

Visiting

fondly. We are happy to see how you have progressed with therapy which, of course, is a tribute to your tenacity."

"I am extremely proud of you. My family has heard all about you. They may have missed me on Christmas Eve, 2011. But we all agree I was exactly where I should have been that night. Please give my best regards to your family. They were always with you. I hope 2013 is a great year for you. We would love to hear from you again."

"Sincerely,

Mike Maggart"

CHAPTER 21

Hands

I continued my therapy and found that hand therapy was especially difficult. The only way I can describe the pain is to have you imagine bending your fingers backwards as far as they will bend right before they break. That's how it felt.

For the first six months I cried during every session of hand therapy. It was very embarrassing, but I couldn't help it. There were always other patients around and I am sure it made them uncomfortable. I envied them because none of them ever cried during their therapy session. I just hoped that someday I would get to the point where it was no longer so painful.

Finally, I got to a place in therapy where my therapist, Scot McCoy, couldn't do any more to improve my hands. He suggested surgery.

We went to a hand surgeon, who came highly recommended. He wanted me to have Botox injections before doing any surgery. Botox shots are used to relax the muscles and with any luck it would straighten out my fingers. I had no idea that Botox is used quite often for various medical treatments. I always thought it's only use was for removing wrinkles.

When the Botox didn't work, my hand surgeon said that I would require two surgeries. The first being tendon transfers and the second would be to release the caplets. This was a surgery that I was very anxious to have. I was hoping that it would allow me to have my hands and fingers back the way they were, or at least close. It would all be worth it.

Prior to surgery, my fingers were in a claw like position.

Following my surgery my fingers were comparatively straight.

However, I was in for many months of therapy just to maintain what I had. The therapy sessions were much easier following my surgery, I no longer cried. Not only was therapy easier for me, but it was easier for Rod and Scot as well. I know how difficult it must have been for both of them to see me in tears every time I had therapy. We all knew that it was a necessary evil, one that we couldn't get around, but none of us enjoyed the experience.

Scot and Rod are both natural comedians, so they would crack jokes throughout my sessions. They were very spontaneous and fed off of each other. This was a way for them to take my mind off of the pain I experienced. It was a diversion that worked fairly well.

My hands had prevented me from doing so many things that I was so used to doing. Because of the special utensils I had to use because of the difficulty with my grasp, I had to keep a fork in our vehicle so when we decided to go out to eat, on the spur of the moment, I would have my special fork available. Granted this was just a minor inconvenience compared to everything else that I was dealing with, but I was reminded of it at every meal.

Following the surgery on my right hand, I had to wait ten months to have surgery on my left hand. The surgeon wanted to wait and see how I progressed with my right hand before he would agree to do surgery on my left hand. This turned out to be another set of months that dragged on with seemingly no end in sight.

Keeping me going was the knowledge that with the use of my hands I would be able to dress myself, I would be able to sign my name for the first time in three years. I would no longer have to take my mug with a handle every place that I went. I would be able to hold a glass in my hand like everyone else.

I would have some of my independence back.

As it was, I had to think about everything I was going to do ahead of time and take my "special needs" items with me. If we were going to travel, I would have to make sure that I went to the bathroom prior to leaving because I was unable to pull my pants up and down. I was limited to how much I could drink because Rod couldn't go into the restroom with me in public places. If we were lucky, some places would provide a "family" restroom, but they were few and far between. When there were no family restrooms and I couldn't wait, we would have to make an exception.

Rod ended up going into the ladies room with me on more than one occasion when I just couldn't wait any longer. I know it was very difficult for him to have to do this, but there were times that we just didn't have a choice.

CHAPTER 22

Post Parkinson and Dystonia

In addition to the issues with my hands, I had stiffness throughout my body. When I walked, my movements were robotic. Normally when a person walks, their arms sway. My arms, however, were stiff and didn't move. I had no idea what was causing the stiffness, so I asked my rehabilitation doctor if she could help me. She suggested I see a movement specialist.

I waited three months to get in to see Dr. Moguel, a neurologist who specialized in movement disorders. He requested all of my medical records, which included a CAT scan of my brain. After reviewing my medical history and doing a few tests in his office, Dr. Moguel announced that

I had Post Parkinson's Disease and Dystonia. This meant I had involuntary muscle contractions that cause repetitive or twisting movement as well as stiffness. He said that secondary Parkinson's means that I was not born with this condition, but rather acquired it through a medical condition (the aortic dissection).

Dr. Moguel gave me a lot of hope when I asked him if he could help me and he said, "Yes." Needless to say, I was thrilled.

He put me on a regimen of a couple of different medications that are used to treat Parkinson's disease. He warned me of the side effects, including nausea, which should only last approximately two weeks. As difficult as it was, I worked through it and the nausea finally subsided in the expected time. I knew I had to see if this medication was going to be my miracle drug. It would be a small price to pay if it worked. The other drug he prescribed could cause memory loss. But again, I had to give it a try.

After having been on this medication for several months, I noticed only a slight change. I hadn't given up because Dr. Moguel said that if these particular medications didn't help, he had others he would try.

While we had to try, unfortunately it turned out that none of the medications worked. I was devastated.

Post Parkinson and Dystonia

Dr. Miguel had one more idea.

He suggested that I try DBS surgery (Deep Brain Stimulation). The surgery works with patients who were born with Parkinson's disease, and to a lesser extent people with post Parkinson's. After appealing time after time and receiving denial after denial from the insurance company, I had no place to turn, as the price of the surgery was approximately $120,000.

Unfortunately, this was not an option for us to pay out of pocket.

So for now, until medical science comes up with my medical miracle, I will live my life to the fullest!

Conclusion

When we enter this world there are no guarantees that we will live a full and happy life. In fact, most of us will experience things in our lives that we wish we didn't have to go through. Some things that I have been through in my life were no fault of my own. The molestation, my son's cancer, and the aortic dissection were all life-changing events that I had no control over.

Other situations that I was involved in, I did have control over, but I made some very bad decisions. I should have never stayed with an abusive husband and I should have never married an alcoholic. These are things that I will always regret.

I have learned many things from these bad decisions. If you are in an abusive relationship, get out of it immediately, especially if you have children. One of the biggest regrets

I have is knowing that my children had to witness my abuse for so long. If you don't have children, do not bring any into the situation. It absolutely will not make things better. Look for a support system whether it be family or friends or even a co-worker.

Don't ever let your pride or fear get in your way of doing what you need to do.

Don't believe an abuser. They will tell you again and again how sorry they are and how it will never happen again, but it always does happen again and again. Don't think that you will ever change them. You won't.

As far as the molestation goes, tell somebody, and don't stop telling them until you are heard. If they still won't listen, tell someone else. Also realize that it is not your fault. It took me going to a therapist later in my life to learn and understand this. I would encourage anyone who has been molested to seek help through a therapist or other professional. Believe in yourself. I never knew the strength that was inside of me until I was on my own and saw that I could not only succeed, but thrive.

Life definitely threw me a curve ball when I had the aortic dissection. I never imagined that I would ever have to be faced with the obstacles that I now have before me. I know that it is something that I can overcome. My drive and determination have allowed me to persevere through

Conclusion

some of the most difficult situations throughout my life. Getting through this will be no different. With the love and support from my family and especially my husband Rod, I have no doubt that I will be able to lead a long and fulfilling life.

While I was in the coma in Tennessee, I remember having a thought that came to me asking me if I wanted to stay, or did I want to go? I don't remember seeing anyone. It was someone working through my thoughts. I do believe that this question came from God, asking me if I wanted to go on living or not. While shocked, I answered, "Hell no, I don't want to go, I'm too young to go."

I wouldn't be here if it wasn't for God. I do believe that I am one of God's miracles. I also believe in the power of prayer. I literally had hundreds of people praying for me. I now know that when I die, I will be going to heaven, because it does exist.

Instead of being angry at God, I feel very blessed. I know that there is a reason that he let me live. Although I don't know yet what his plan is for me, I know that it will come to me before I leave this world.

I am now approaching the five year mark of when my world was turned upside down with the aortic dissection. Although I have made a lot of progress, I still have a long way to go. I believe that the spirit within me will have a profound impact on the journey that I am on, through the rest of my life.

Rod is now retired and we have a lot of plans going forward. We love to travel and have many places to see on our bucket list. We still plan to buy a cabin near a lake, sit on the front porch and watch the sunset. I will never let my limitations define me.

I know that God gave me a second chance at life for a reason. Maybe, just maybe, my book will be an inspiration to someone who can relate to some of the things that I have been through. I hope it will give them the courage and strength to fight through their situation and ultimately find peace in their life. If my book will inspire just one person, it will all be worth it.

Acknowledgments

Dodds Tyler, who introduced me to Rod, the love of my life. He gave me the greatest gift ever. Without him introducing us, I can't imagine where my life would be today, and for that I am truly grateful.

I always knew that I had a lot of good friends, but I didn't realize the impact they would have on my recovery. They rallied around me at a time when I needed them the most. Barb and Kevin McCann, Shawn and Rhonda Young, Jennifer and Marty McMannis, Lynn Sebo, Debbe LaPeirre, and TJ (Theresa) Kuleff continue to be my cheerleaders.

Lynn, Debbe, and TJ took turns taking care of our basset hounds, Ernest T and Charlene, while I was in the hospital in Tennessee. For that, I am forever grateful.

The Spirit Within Me

Linda Angel Simmons lives in Knoxville, which is in the same city as Parkwest Hospital. While I was in a coma, my sister Brenda asked her if she would visit me during the time when she had to go back to Nebraska. Not only did she visit me every day, but often she would visit twice a day. She would read to me and once in awhile she would sing. I will never forget what she did for me. That is why I call her "My angel girl" even today.

Our friends, Larry and Laurie Hermann, presented us with a check which we used to purchase our new sectional sofa. Our old sofa had a manual lever in order to recline and I wasn't able to operate it with my hands the way they were. Our new sofa has an electric button to push, so that I can recline. This provided me with the freedom to get up and down from my recliner without assistance.

My family has been incredible. My sister Brenda and her husband Rick Walkowiak made numerous trips back and forth from Omaha, Nebraska to Tennessee while I was in the hospital. My sons, Daniel and Mike, drove from Arizona to Tennessee and stayed for three weeks. My brother Keith flew to Arizona to help me after shoulder surgery, while Rod was at work. My step-daughter Jenn and her husband Enan Parezo traveled seven hours from South Carolina to visit me while I was still in the hospital. Paul and Tiff, my step-son and his wife, took care of our house while we were in Tennessee.

Conclusion

My mom and dad, Larry and Jackie Crew, were always there for me. They never gave up. They always believed I would pull through, even when one of the doctors said, "What you see, is what you get."

My nephew, Jon Laubert, gave us a check after learning that we had to pay for the medical jet out of pocket, in order for me to get me back home to Arizona. We could never thank him enough.

My Aunt Linda and Uncle Michael Vine bought me a Samsung tablet, which I put to good use. I used it to write my book!

I have Dr. Maggart to thank for saving my life. He will always be my hero. The staff at Parkwest Hospital and St Joseph's Hospital were fantastic. I had outstanding care. My therapists, Scot McCoy and Sara Derosa, here in Arizona, are the best of the best! I am forever grateful.

I can't say enough about my husband Rod. He is my rock. I really don't know what I would do without him. He has been there when I needed a soft place to land. He always finds a way to lift me up when I am feeling down. The past four years have been extremely difficult, not only for me, but for Rod as well. He was juggling so much, taking me to doctor visits, therapy three days a week and going to work. He was definitely burning the candle at both ends. He now knows how to use a blow dryer and a flat iron. For

The Spirit Within Me

everything that we have been through, we still love each other unconditionally.

Made in the USA
Middletown, DE
12 February 2017